# Make

# MONEY

# Online

Ways To Make (And Save Money) Online: Affiliate Marketing, Dropshipping, Shopify, Blog, Self Publishing, Selling Online Video Courses, Handicrafts, And More

## AMY LANDRY

# SOMMARIO

# CHAPTER I PASSIVE INCOME

Living on an income ... having a passive income ... a passive income ... passive income ... lying on a beautiful beach with a cool cocktail in hand and earning without doing anything, even while you sleep ... that's what comes to your mind, right?

There is nothing wrong with this but you must immediately understand that living on an income thanks to passive income, being free financially, means only that you can afford not to be always productive and no longer have to depend on a professional income.

It therefore means having total control over your finances and your time.

It means doing what you want often when you want, it means having a lot of free time... but it doesn't mean not doing anything anymore.

Personally, it is for these latter reasons that I began to explore the economic and financial world many years ago when I learned that the key to living on an income lay in the concept of passive income.

Then it took me 7 years of great commitment and many attempts to learn how the "system" worked, and then to acquire mastery of it, up to having full control.

It may not be a definitive status because some opportunities capable of generating passive income may be limited in time and therefore it is necessary to be aware that it may be necessary to update one's sources of passive income even when certain results have been achieved.

Therefore, those who think they can constantly stay sitting in the sun from morning to evening just because they have understood how to generate passive income, can safely stop reading ... because they are deluded or because someone has told them that this is so!

*So, let's start talking about how to make more money by not working, than how much you can make by working.*

Like many, I initially thought of passive income exclusively as something that once activated would function and self-regenerate without any intervention from me.

I found this idea intoxicating. The idea of traveling the world and sunning myself on many beautiful islets while money did everything by itself was what attracted me most... too bad that all this, exactly in these terms, is not so easily achievable.

I want to be clear; you can certainly live off passive income and live very well... but this requires work, "maintenance" and, sometimes, the need to regenerate or recreate alternative sources of income that could run out.

Of course, it's much better than working in a factory or being enslaved in the office for a few euros ... but it is right that you know that this is not all and it is not always perpetual automatism.

All this to tell you that the crux of passive income is that it allows you first of all to free up your time from work to dedicate it to doing things that, although less demanding, are more profitable.

Most of the people who have freed themselves financially and who live off their passive income do not spend all day in a Ferrari in Monte Carlo or on a Polynesian beach (these are the visions generated by some for the poor fools to pluck. ...) but they spend their time making their passive income sources work as well as studying new opportunities or pursuing their passions, as well as their hobbies.

Therefore, remember that the beauty of living on a passive income consists first of all in being able to free your time from work to dedicate it to much more interesting or much more profitable things.

If you have the ambition and the courage to be able to think of getting out of the rat race, creating passive income, you must be clear that when you succeed, you are able to live on an income, have a good life, because first of all you can afford to do only what you love or are passionate about.

When passive income supports your standard of living, you will also want to do something with a higher and nobler meaning and purpose. You will see that it will be like this ...

Writing books, traveling, learning, creating start-ups, spending more time with your children, doing good works for those who really need it, helping others to follow your path, you will find your higher purpose ...

Sure, you might as well spend more time making more money, but that will become an option, a choice, not a necessity anymore.

### FANTASTIC, ISN'T IT?

It is, but to get to this, believe me, it takes commitment, learning, dedication and you have to have the right experiences, even make mistakes.

## The Law of Passive Income

There are many possibilities to access passive income and I don't think there is anyone able to innovate something in this sense as there is no hidden secret. Who tells you the opposite ... only tells you lies!

My thoughts on this aspect are aimed at making clear how profitable businesses are generated (possibly passive and systematized), how the economy and above all finance works.

So, let's start from the basics to establish some general rules on renting and passive income.

## Money is generated where Real Value is created

Value is what constitutes advantage / benefit / utility / result for people who are willing to pay to obtain or use it.

**Seems very basic in approach, doesn't it?**

It is, but most people don't seem to understand this crucial step.

Whenever someone receives money, it means that some value has been created and that someone has decided to pay for it. The first issue you need to focus on is therefore: creating value.

An employee also creates value. He does this, for example, by moving goods into a warehouse or entering purchase orders or by doing the billing for payroll. The employer then buys from him those services which are of value to him.

The employee is consequently paid according to a simple formula: Income = Time x Value.

However, time is a limited resource (6-12 hours). This is why everyone tries, consciously or not, to act on the second variable, the value.

### How?

For example, graduating or trying to do an MBA with the aim of getting paid more for their value for the same time.

Yet, in the end, even reaching the maximum earning potential for one's Value, the limit will once again be Time.

Therefore, Time will always limit your income because time is not expandable and you cannot create it as you can Value.

### So, what can you do?

First of all, you must be clear that Value that can only be consumed only once or rarely is never enough.

You are precious. Your time, your work, your knowledge, your experience, it's all worth something. In fact, your employer or your clients, whether you are a professional or an entrepreneur, pay to get it.

*The problem is that, if you are an employee, your value always equals the same income ...*

In fact, even if you are a surgeon, a lawyer, an artist, an engineer, or even a baker, often the value you create is often consumed only from time to time and with a certain rarity. You can only sell one loaf of bread to the same customer at a time. You can only sell one open heart surgery to a client. You can only follow one divorce for a client...

### Are you there?

So, you have to understand that one of the key principles of passive income is to break this relationship, to create value that many people can enjoy at the same time and that can be sold over and over again.

Value is created by people, but it does not necessarily have to be the same people who sell or supply it.

Value is always created by a human being. However, who says it must be the human being himself who has to provide that value?

Some human beings, undoubtedly capable, have created value by conceiving Google, but they are certainly not the ones who provide it to you. They are not the ones who directly provide you with the results of a search or a map.

Your landlord has worked to buy the apartment you live in and also to find you as a tenant. Now that you have chosen his value, however, all he has to do is receive monthly compensation for the value you have chosen, without having to provide you with another apartment.

Again ... if you create something for which you can ask for a "monthly fee" you will have generated value only once to continue to receive passive income automatically.

**You start to understand, right?**

## Passive income is not free money

We can therefore define passive income as those income-generating activities that are not dependent (or are marginally dependent) on your commitment in terms of Time.

*This is very nice but... to create such a value it takes commitment and time!*

We can therefore speak of living on rent and true passive income, only where we have separated (or at least severely limited) the proportional relationship between the time spent and the money earned, in other words, the gain must be very high, not necessarily in an absolute sense. but it certainly must be with respect to the time taken.

*Now I really think you understand the concept perfectly, right?*

The three types of value to be considered in order to live on an income

## Selling Value

The term "sale" probably does not need much explanation and is associated with situations, in principle, where the value is transferred only once (or very rarely) in exchange for money. Any professional activity, for example, is therefore a way to sell value.

This obviously, in terms of passive income, is not optimal, because once you make a sale to a customer, you can't immediately resell the same advice, it will take some time to do so and, in some cases, it may not even be more possible.

However, if I could make of that same competence / experience / specialization that I used to sell a consultancy, for example, a book or a digital product (e-book, video course...), here, with perhaps a marginal cost, I could sell my value over and over again without having to do it directly.

## Renting Value

By renting something, you can generally avoid the degradation of its value, or at least decrease it as well as obtain a passive income from it. You just have to realize that, if you rent an apartment, the value you are offering is not the house itself but the refuge, the comfort, the safety...

The more value you give to these items, the more money you can earn from that property.

Make **MONEY** *Online*

## Earning with an Indirect Value

The indirect value is similar, in terms of modality, to the sale or rental value but differs in some substantial aspects.

To put it simply, here too, let's give an example ...

Let's say you create a blog, where the value is the information, it contains. For this, however, readers pay nothing. However, with this blog I may have created a powerful form of indirect value: the attention and following of readers.

I could then rent this value to advertisers, who pay, on a regular basis, to be visible to my readers.

**You there yet?**

## Engineering of annuity living and passive income

Knowing now that there are many ways to create value, and what they are, you now simply need to look at the cost / benefit ratio of each in order to be selective about how to create your own value. You must therefore create or purchase resources that offer value "automatically". In essence, in building your plan to make a living, you need to consider what you can create or acquire to have value that can be easily and repeatedly "passed on" to others with as little work and the least amount of time as possible.

This is therefore the meaning of the term "passive": obtaining income by doing as little as possible, the bare minimum.

There are, as mentioned, a ton of ways to do this, but they all fall into the 3 categories above.

**So, let's go into a little more detail, ok?**

## Digital products, software, infoproducts, photos / videos / music tracks...

This area includes many elements, from electronic books to images to online training courses. It is therefore a question of creating a digital product that has value.

**Why digital?**

Sure, if you make handmade sweaters, you make something very beautiful but you can't just duplicate and resell them. Also, you need to wrap, pack and ship them. Nothing wrong with that, of course, but this means that there is a relationship between work and income, and we have already seen the reason why this is not ideal.

Digital goods, on the other hand, are infinitely and simply duplicable and you can design systems (or use online platforms) to supply everything automatically.

Finally, if it is software, nowadays it is very often an App. You do not need to be a software developer but you need to know who to contact because you need someone who can, in addition to creating the App, also worry about making the necessary updates and to intervene in case of problems.

## Patents

If you're smart or creative enough to create something patentable, go for it!

This requires commitment and work in many aspects, including legal ones, but if someone asks you to be able to take advantage of what you have created, you are guaranteed a passive income for as long as they use it.

## Blog, YouTube channel, Information material...

I have deliberately separated this aspect from the first point because here I am referring in particular to the creation of indirect value.

As mentioned, if you can create a popular blog that many well-profiled readers read continuously (just think of fashion or food bloggers...) it is possible to sell advertising space or be compensated for a series of visual contributions, sponsorships or citations.

Alternatively, if you create a more niche but highly thematic / specialist blog, you can operate on affiliations. It is about offering links to websites and getting paid when people buy from those sites through those links.

You just have to consider that, this is passive income only when the time you spend writing the content is minimal compared to the earnings or, another possibility, when it is others who write the content for you but you enjoy the real benefits.

For example, there are those who have involved writers in their projects and then only worry about investing their time for SEO (positioning on search engines) by detecting the keywords to have the right topics to deal with. Others do just the opposite. Still others do neither, that is, they have automated everything.

Do you mean that it is possible to automate all of this? Yes, all this is now almost entirely automatable.

## Sale of real products

As we said earlier, there is nothing passive about this, except if you are unable to create a fully automated business, including customer service and shipping. If you want to learn more about this, find out, for example, about dropshipping activities.

## Properties

Even if, unlike what we saw previously, real estate often requires a minimum of economic availability, the real estate sector is always a good resource to live on an income. Furthermore, there is still the possibility of creating passive income by exploiting the money of a bank, thus using the leverage effect.

It is true that if you do not have your own capital, part of the money will go into mortgage, as well as taxes and insurance but in the meantime, you create a fortune. If you want to invest in real estate then you must know how to buy very well, because it is in the purchase that you can make the difference.

You can rent properties in the traditional way or even do it daily / weekly thanks to platforms such as Airbnb. In this case, however, you must consider elements such as the time for the delivery of the keys or pre and post rental cleaning.

## Financial investments

Stocks, bonds, investment funds, ETFs... can produce passive income as long as you invest to seek "dividends".

These can be great generators of passive income, because knowing how to act and understanding the logic of time and compound interest, these are low-risk investments.

Also, on this I avoid dwelling.

## Investing in start-ups or company shares

It involves investing in new business ventures or existing businesses to earn part of the profits.

I do not want to go further on this issue because, before thinking about this, it is better if you pass from being a professional or an entrepreneur and from having done it even with some success.

I only told you about it because part of my passive income today derives from being a (non-operating) shareholder of some companies.

## Diversification

As mentioned at the beginning, even by freeing yourself financially, it is not certain that you can completely stop working because some opportunities that generate passive income are unfortunately limited in time.

Also, more than half of what people try to do doesn't produce results. In this sense and compared to living on an income, diversification is your best ally.

Having multiple sources of passive income, in addition to a professional income (maybe finally linked only to what you love to do), you will have your correct strategy, hedged from any risk.

*Conclusions on your chances of living on an annuity thanks to passive income*

Like any methodology to get more with less, to make a living on an income, there are aspects that you need to consider and address. I have already listed and explained some of these to you, but I'd better tell you a few more things:

## Passive income is not created passively

You have to work hard to get it. After all, even those who ask for thousands of euros to have surgery have done a great deal before getting there. Only after this phase can you then think of getting to work a few hours a day or a week.

***Passive income also means doing things you don't love excessively***

I'll explain...

To generate passive income, you need perseverance and determination and you may also need to learn and do things that you do not particularly appreciate or that are outside your comfort zone or that will require, as far as you are concerned, a lot of effort.

The point is, however, that you have to make enough money before you can only do what you want.

Passive Income or Passive Earnings does not necessarily replace active income

If you free yourself financially by being able to live on an income, you don't necessarily stop working.

### Why?

*Simple: Because you might even get bored doing nothing!*

*Not all passive income will always remain passive*

As mentioned, many passive incomes wear out over time or need to be regenerated because some types of passive income are subject to competition. For this reason, even when financial freedom has been achieved, we must remain vigilant. That's why I enjoy creating and always looking for new strategies for new passive income channels. The advantage is that, in this research and testing / verification process, I have more time to dedicate to it than most of the people I know have. You cannot build a successful business without skill and without working hard.

**What does this have to do with it?**

For your passive income, unless you are already a Professional or an Entrepreneur, start first from:

- financial investments that produce dividends
- digital business based on your great passions / interests or on your competence / experience / specialization
- real estate to be used as income.

*"Yes, ok but I can't do all this because I don't have a saleable value ..."*

Everyone can have (or can create) saleable value. It can be more or less difficult, but to say I can't because I don't have... it's just an excuse, an alibi. I tell you frankly... this is the typical excuse of the poor and of losers.

*"But is it possible to have enough passive income to sustain a high standard of living?"*

It depends on what you mean by high standard of living. If you intend to have yachts and Ferraris by living in Monte Carlo and dining on champagne, lobster, oysters and caviar every night then you may need to have an active income as well.

If, on the other hand, you mean ... still living very well, traveling, making your passions a job, having a lot of free time, enjoying life and having much more fun than the vast majority of people do ... then you can certainly live on an income, supporting all this with your passive income.

# CHAPTER 2 AFFILIATE MARKETING

Affiliate Marketing or Performance
Marketing is one of the rising disciplines
of digital marketing.

Among all the available channels, Affiliate Marketing stands out because it is the best-known performance channel and it represents a new form, started online, of highly successful digital marketing. Being a powerful channel, very widespread but also quite complex in its genre, it is necessary first of all to define your goals, get information before spending money and finally decide on the best strategy that best suits your business by making the most of the strength of the medium.

Affiliate Marketing is in fact an exclusively performance channel: the advertiser pays only for the results generated by the affiliate program based on the objectives set by himself. Better to say, compared to all other forms of advertising management in digital, it has a completely different model of commercial engagement: you pay for the sale and you don't pay for the space.

Performance Marketing is a promotional channel that is part of the new forms of online marketing.

## It consists of a commercial agreement between three parties:

The first person is the merchant or advertiser who promotes an affiliate program to recruit publishers or affiliates to promote their online business.

The second subject is the publisher or affiliate who participates in the affiliate program by registering their website, portal or web property by entering the JavaScript code that will host the advertisements. Subsequently, the publisher, through search engine optimization (SEO) and search engine marketing (SEM) promotion activities, will acquire traffic on its web site by promoting the merchant's advertisements together with its own content.

The third party is the affiliation platform, that is the party that provides the know-how and technology to manage payments, exchange advertising material and resolve disputes between the various publishers.

## Technical characteristics of an affiliate program

Analyzing in depth the technical characteristics of an effective affiliate program, it is good to keep in mind some elements such as an incentive payout (distribution of net profits in the form of dividends), restrictive but protective policies for the best performing publishers and captivating creative formats. The types of payment adopted by the affiliate platform respect the characteristics of the promotional channel, that is, exclusively for performance and require a tracking system to protect the promotional work done by publishers.

The tracking is carried out with JavaScript encodings that generate types of payment such as CPC and CPM, or the attribution of the compensation for the purchase generated days after the click made and the impression found. This is a practice refined over the years that today seems to be the most widespread and most appreciated by publishers.

The difference between Affiliate Marketing and classic Internet Marketing consists in receiving compensation only after an action carried out on the affiliate's site (CPA = Cost per Action, CPL = Cost per Lead) and other forms of CPC remuneration and CPM.

## Relationship between Advertisers, Platforms and Publishers

The remuneration model of Affiliate Marketing is therefore mainly that of:

- CPA or cost per action - goes on a per cart basis and is a percentage
- CPL or cost per lead - is represented by a fixed cost

In addition to the pure affiliate remuneration models mentioned above there are also:

- CPM or cost per thousand impressions - or views, is widely used to make brand awareness
- CPC or cost per click - the remuneration is triggered when the user clicks and lands on the merchant's site

Let's take a closer look at this business relationship by taking some simple examples.

The affiliate relationship is a so-called win-win relationship: I, as an advertiser, have to advertise to promote a product / service, to make a purchase, to have someone register on my site. As a publisher, I have to deliver advertising so if I made the user do the action, I won: because you will pay me a commission. If I managed to get the action done, I won, because I have an economic return. Obviously, the affiliate platform acting as an intermediary will also have an ROI.

In essence, Affiliate Marketing is a relationship which is not based on the principle of advertising delivery, but on the commercial relationship: I, as an advertiser, make my publishers my sales force. Put simply, I give you advertising material and you have to publish and sell it for me. Transported to the real world it is as if, for example, I asked some people to make flyers for me, making sure that I will pay them for every entrance I have in my club. However, since the world of Affiliate Marketing is all digital, here we will only have purely technical web materials, entirely mediated by technology.

As we said before, the affiliate platform must also have a remuneration. Taking a simple example in the real world, it is as if I, the owner, wanted to earn on the entrances to my restaurant through flyers, rather than dealing with it personally, I asked someone to find me the best flyers and I assured the person in charge a good and high percentage of compensation on all the successful leafleting activities of those employees.

Within the characteristics of Affiliate Marketing, the concept of intermediation as a standard works like this in most cases: after making a profit, the advertiser offers the publisher 70% of the commission. 30% of the commission goes to the affiliate platform. Taking an example in figures, if I establish as an advertiser that for every €100, I earn thanks to this marketing activity I will have to give this affiliate system, formed by the platform and publishers, €10 for every €100, I will give €7 to the publisher and €3 to the platform.

However, it is not a fixed rule in the commission system, there are situations where it can happen that the affiliate platform chooses to recognize itself much less, such as 10% or 5% of the commission. It happens if we are talking about customers, advertisers, of very high calibre who produce huge turnover, who have great ability to scale the costs of the affiliate system in an important way.

## Manage an affiliate program

Managing an Affiliate Program is a more complex process than it may initially seem, so let's keep these things in mind:

An Affiliate Network is not a black hole in which we place advertisements and receive money;

The Affiliate Marketing program is first of all a consultative process towards the advertiser: if a program does not work it is likely that something has gone wrong in this process;

Publishers must be managed and the best performing ones must be recognized in order to promote the program to them;

Affiliates constitute a "sales force" to be constantly encouraged. It is necessary to activate promotions and "competitions" between publishers;

Publishers apply to participate in the program; screening must be done at least once a week to keep the program alive;

In a successful program, the queue of publishers can be long, it is necessary to constantly monitor the activity of each of them, some could implement borderline methodologies that do not generate any value and actually correspond to scams;

It is necessary to periodically check the validity of the generated sales / leads and possibly proceed with the cancellation of those that are not valid in order not to pay affiliates for actions that do not correspond to a revenue for the advertiser.

## The 15 steps to launch an Affiliate Program

Agree with the advertiser the action(s) to be remunerated, the commission and the need to use a landing page or not;

Create the program on the platform, generate the tracking codes and, if required, set the platform to deliver the creatives;

Launch the program with a newsletter to all publishers subscribed to the platform, so that they learn about the new program;

Recruit the best performing publishers relevant to the type of advertiser;

Screen publishers who have applied to the program (once a week);

Monitor the results;

Plan publisher incentive actions;

Verify the actions and eventual cancellation of the fake (1 - 2 times a month);

Perform actions of constant renewal of creativity;

Schedule communication to affiliates about promotions and any opportunities to increase results.

## The KPIs of Performance Marketing

Affiliate Marketing is used to generate immediate and measurable results such as:

- Sales
- Leads

It is the most efficient marketing medium in digital today. If used well it requires:

- Building a solid affiliate base
- Daily and granular management

Contrary to popular belief, the affiliates who bring results, as we will see, are not those who use the display adv medium.

Finally, it is a tool that can suffer in terms of effectiveness:

- If the brand / product is not well known
- If the product is not palatable

## The Affiliate Program cycle

To really understand how the affiliate system works, let's look at it from the point of view not as an employee, but as a user. Let's say that we normally browse a site, but with more or less interest as a consumer. As we scroll through news and articles, we come across advertisements. Such advertisements may or may not catch our attention. If they manage to capture it, they potentially earn our click and end up on the merchant's or advertiser's site. Furthermore, if we decide to buy an item on the same site, a virtuous circle is created that starts from our first click and then from our first entry, ending up with a sale. What happens then? We took part in a real commercial transaction cycle.

A technological mechanism was activated by which the advertiser's site called the affiliate platform, which intercepted the type of sale, marking it as made thanks to a click from one of its publishers or advertisers. In this case, the payment notification is triggered for the success of the transaction according to the agreed commissions.

Some well-known brands that effectively use Affiliate Marketing are:

- Amazon and Amazon BuyVIP
- Zalando
- Yoox
- Expedia
- eDreams
- Hotels.com

They essentially use it to get highly qualified results for their business.

## How to Start Affiliate Marketing

When it comes to affiliate marketing, we are fascinated by the potential that this sector offers, in terms of earnings and flexibility of schedules and locations but we tend to forget that there is a job to do, similar to a path that we can define broadly in these 15 STEPS + Extras.

Becoming a professional affiliate is the dream of many Affiliate Marketing beginners, but being one means facing several challenges and the very first is how to get started right with affiliate marketing.

Above all because the affiliate landscape is dotted with characters (which from now on we will define as GURU) who proclaim themselves as "best affiliate marketers", "number one in the affiliate", "the reference point of Italian affiliate marketing" and so on. With testimonies of people who seem to be under blackmail and who do not say what they sell and with what methods.

For this reason, I recommend that you stay away from such characters and start reading this short guide to get started with affiliate marketing without making mistakes (and wasting money and time).

# Make MONEY Online

## STEP 1: What do you like to do?

Start with Affiliate Marketing from your passions, ask yourself: "What do I like to do?" What pleasantly takes your time?

If you can identify your passions, you will find the niche to start working on. When you talk about a topic that you like, it certainly doesn't weigh on you, you want to study, investigate, test and above all know your potential competition well. It will allow you to understand who your competitors are and what problems the users of that niche have, because you are the first to be a user who has problems (and has had them in the past) and has found a way to solve them.

Especially if you are at the beginning, I advise you to work on your passions for a simple reason: you could fail because if you work in a niche that you know little about and that you are not passionate about, you will imagine the wishes and problems of users, you will turn to users who probably do not do what they are interested in.

## STEP 2: Register a domain

Once you have identified a niche, to create a website you need to register a domain. There are many services that allow you to register one from € 8 to € 30 per year, depending on how much space and what services you order.

I recommend that you use the domain name for the major search keywords you intend to rank for.

For example, if you want to talk about children's toys, try to register the domain giocattoliperbambini .it / toysforchildren.com /.eu /.info /.net /.org or other free domains. Don't make the mistake of registering a long, hardly rememberable domain name. Do not choose a fancy name and remember that it must be in line with the main keyword, easy to remember, easily readable and that it can become a brand.

The domain extension (.com or .eu) is not important for the positioning.

## STEP 3: Create a website or blog

If you intend to create a blog in WordPress (which I recommend, for reliability and ease of use) you will need to purchase a linux hosting plan with database. Some offer a pre-installed wordpress package, others allow you with wizard to install WordPress in less than 5 minutes.

The only care you must have is to install it on the root of the domain and not in a folder or subdomain.

Choose a functional and beautiful theme, install the basic plugins: Antispam, SEO, Cache, contact form and other plugins suitable for your needs.

Create the pages: Who we are (or who I am), contacts, privacy policy and cookie law, obviously the latter based on the use of data.

## STEP 4: Write content

Start writing content, original and useful. Provide the solutions to users who need to read the article, solutions that you have tested and which work.

The user needs practical advice, he does not want to waste time.

Don't be afraid to express your ideas, to write and to compare yourself with other users.

Each of us is good at doing something, blogging can be useful for other users to face some things and for ourselves to learn to communicate.

## STEP 5: Create community

Communities may seem like a waste of time but they are actually a great source of content.

Through communities you can understand what users want, what they dream of, what they love and what they hate. You can talk to them and it could be a way to study and delve into other topics before providing an answer.

It can also be a stimulus to organize dedicated events and content.

NEVER look at your communities as a source of income, remember that they are people like you and even if they decide to give you money, they will have to do it freely.

You can create communities through Forum, facebook group, Telegram or through e-mail database.

## STEP 6: Insert the first advertisements

Get started with Google AdSense and Amazon. Amazon to understand how to technically insert text links (avoid putting graphic banners) and AdSense to understand how much your pages are worth and what kind of advertisers could be interested in your pages.

Don't go overboard with ad slots, remember:

The user is on your site for content and not to mistakenly click on an advertisement!

Engaging in these two partnerships will allow you to be more credible in the eyes of affiliate networks and future advertisers.

## STEP 7: Curate the social channels

Each social channel has its purpose and you need to communicate, even the same concept, differently.

Never be obvious or trivial and offer value. Those who decide to follow you must do so because they trust you, can receive something and can donate something: the concept of knowledge I told you about in the community.

Social channels can help you communicate better, such as Instagram Stories to express concepts quickly and increase the ability to synthesize. Use LIVE on Facebook to connect with your users, YouTube to learn how to communicate in video, LinkedIn to offer value in the workplace.

You don't have to use all social media, better to use a few but good ones and they can be used to increase your authority in the sector.

Authoritativeness cannot be bought, it is a recognition that users give based on content, reliability and availability.

## STEP 8: Register on the affiliate networks

This step is very important because your affiliate career depends on this choice. Do not follow easy earnings and feeding junk to your users, seriously consider working with big brands!

For this reason, I recommend that you register with the best European affiliate networks, which manage well-known brands and require a professional working method.

I would recommend: Awin, Tradedoubler, TradeTracker and FinanceAds (if you are dealing with financial products).

To be accepted by these affiliate networks it is necessary to respect the quality standard. You must:

- Have the website registered in your name.
- The website must be related to a category or niche, avoid submitting consulting sites.
- NO adult, porn, violence, and avoid submitting sites on weight loss.

## STEP 9: request the offers that interest you

The affiliate networks that I have suggested have many advertisers divided by category, try to select only advertisers related to your content and not choose them based on pay. Because you would have a hard time putting them in context and they would not accept your application.

Most advertisers accept affiliates and view posted websites. So, if you have a site that talks about pets, avoid applying to credit institutions and car insurance companies, you risk passing for an affiliate marketing amateur and networks will see you as a waste of time.

While you may apply for pet insurance and accessories and food insurance for a booming industry like pet care.

## STEP 10: Affiliate marketing with text links

Avoid using banners or graphic creatives! If you really want to use them, because they are dynamic and indicate current prices, circumscribe them to an exact point to make those advertisements and text links look like opportunities.

Use text links on recognizable links or CTA (Call-To-Action) inviting the user to action with simple and intuitive links.

At the base of Affiliate Marketing is the referral link. Especially for affiliate marketing beginners the referral link is a way to get started. Referral link stands for referring a customer through a unique and tracked link. Generally on many affiliate programs there is the "invite a friend" section which is often considered as an advantage that turns into benefits such as: discounts, vouchers or amazon vouchers. But it is none other than Affiliate Marketing. There is no better way to start.

## STEP 11: Create value for your users

You don't have to think about how much you can earn before embarking on an online project with affiliations, also because it can go wrong but it can also go very well, you can greatly exceed your expectations.

***But one thing must always be clear: you must offer value.***

A value that only you can give, through your history, person and experience.

Communicate what moves you, what is behind your choices and why you decide to use a product or service rather than another. Disconnect from referrals (do not show your users that you recommend something just because you receive a commission) because if you do it free from referrals, when you communicate value, users will be able to recognize the referral and will pay you back 100 times!

At this point I would also like to add a tip: if you deal with marketing do not treat your users as stupid, do not apply marketing techniques on them. They may recognize them and feel offended for making fun of their intelligence.

## STEP 12: Analyze and make decisions

Analyze every step of the process, simplify and reshape your decisions, every day. If you want to be better than your competitors, you cannot leave anything to chance.

Use the analysis tools, there are many on the market: "how do users find you?" , "What do they do on your pages?", "Where do they come from?", "How long do they stay on your page?", "Where do they leave?" - basically you have to know the whole acquisition process and understand where users leave and why.

Only in this way can you improve and offer easy, fast, intuitive and performing solutions.

Learn to do analysis even if you are a beginner in affiliate marketing, precisely because it is an activity that will serve you even when you are in an advanced stage, so for your own good it is better if you start immediately to understand what happens, by doing analysis, and as data and experience grow you will know how to manage critical issues, quickly find solutions and make the right decisions.

## STEP 13: Paid traffic sources

Learn, when you're ready, to use all paid traffic sources: Google Ads, Facebook Ads, DEM, even TikTok Ads!

Don't become dependent on just one traffic source and treat traffic sources as tools to reach potential users.

It is not the tools that make the strategy!

Invest what you can, if initially you don't have enough funds don't think about spending money you don't have, because you could lose it. Work on SEO, learn how to do work on positioning, content, conversion, and analytics, and then reinvest the proceeds from that business into paid traffic.

So, when you get to paid traffic, you will get there with a different skill and awareness.

I understand you might think that this will make you feel like you're wasting precious time, but if you have other options, use them otherwise the alternative to my advice is to give up.

## STEP 14: Conceive Affiliate Marketing as a job

Affiliate Marketing Is a Job!

Not a pastime or an automatic income (also because automatic annuities do not exist) - even to generate income that could be defined automatic you have to work on creation and maintenance, so in the end they have very little that is automatic.

I understand that Affiliate Marketing is approached with the spirit "let's see if this job is for me" but I often see a lot of lightness for online jobs, regardless of whether it is affiliations or something else. A lightness that would not exist in offline work.

Try to give yourself schedules and goals and try to break away from your family, use coworking or dedicated areas, otherwise those around you think that you are wasting time and will interrupt you in a thousand ways.

***And your job will never become a job!***

Affiliate Marketing can give you the concrete possibility to switch from Opportunity Seeker to Digital Entrepreneur.

## STEP 15: Don't be in a hurry

Those who approach affiliations are in a hurry to earn.

In an employee or trainee job you would wait some time before receiving your first salary.

You have the opportunity to learn a job from home and not have excessive costs.

Don't let yourself be ruined by the rush and desire to reach other affiliates' dashboards.

You are investing in your future; take the time you need.

## EXTRA: Diversify

Learn to diversify on:

- projects
- traffic sources
- affiliate networks
- advertisers

If you tie yourself to a product / service you will become an employee of that product or service, ditto for affiliate network, source of traffic and even project.

Start from your passions, create a project, learn how to do it and start on the ground floor. As you need help from outside people, you will be able to quantify the work, pay them and understand its value.

Initially 9 out of 10 projects are unsuccessful. To date the average (fortunately) has improved because I have accumulated experience and vision over the years.

But you have to create, fail and get back up!

## EXTRA: Learn from your mistakes

**Failure Analysis will be your best school.**

Whenever you go wrong, stop, analyze it and find a way to fix it. You will learn from problems and develop problem solving skills. Most of your problems have also happened to other users in the world, learn to use Google, do some research, read and test everything you find.

Especially for those looking for information related to affiliate marketing for beginners and want to understand how to work with affiliations, I would like to suggest an extremely important aspect: analyzing an error will allow you to avoid it in the future.

99% of the problems you solve them with Google and YouTube, 1% with your inventiveness.

## EXTRA: Enjoy and Focus

Don't let others tell you what to do, the hours you will spend on your pc are yours, so try to have fun and stay focused.

Those with an opportunity-seeking disposition see everything that moves as an opportunity, so leave projects that could explode and go back to focus on you.

If you are working on a website for children's footwear and you are well on your way and you are earning like € 400 a month and someone comes along who tells you that with cat brushes, he earns € 12,000 a month. What do you do? You quit your project to find the network that gives you € 20 to sell a cat brush for € 49 which actually costs 5.

***I raise a couple of questions:***

If there is already someone else doing it, you compete with that too.

How much fun is it to peddle brushes for cats for €49? ( I remind you that to justify the cost you have to invent things that are probably not real, people are not stupid, the same brush can be found on Amazon for € 10) - I don't think this way of working is fun.

***What about your project?***

What if I told you that you could earn more money and more time by selling children's shoes than by selling cat brushes?

You probably wouldn't believe me and a stranger's screen would be more believable.

***Do you know why?***

Because deep down, you don't believe in yourself and what you're doing.

We think that working online is about taking what you can today, because who knows how it will go tomorrow. Who knows if users will buy tomorrow or if they will change their habits? So, we think in the short term. It's a mistake I made too and it was a cause for concern when I was working.

The more I found a product / service that was good, the more I understood what I had to do in the short term.

In reality, however, this is not the case. If I am here to talk to you about affiliate marketing after 15 years of doing it as a steady job, I can tell you that I understand that by working in a certain way you will learn to observe and arrive before others on some things. That will be fine for a while but you will always be ahead.

But you have to believe in yourself and what you do.

# Make **MONEY** Online

## CHAPTER 4 DROPSHIPPING

In recent years there has been a slight increase in e-Commerce offering dropshipping, or Drop Ship.

But first of all, what exactly does it mean, how can you start exploiting it, and which are the sites for dropshipping? In this chapter we will clarify these questions, so that you can decide whether to use this sales opportunity for your store.

## What is dropshipping?

Dropshipping is a form of online sales that allows a seller to offer products that they do not physically have in stock.

## How does dropshipping work?

A seller offers some products in his online store. When a customer orders one of these products, the manufacturer himself ships them.

The seller therefore has no physical contact with the product. This e-Commerce strategy is in direct contrast to the classic retail trade, where goods are ordered in large quantities, stored and then shipped to the customer.

In other words: the seller is the intermediary between supplier and customer. The seller takes care of marketing and branding, while the supplier manages the logistics.

***Not sure whether to use dropshipping for your online business?***

At this point you will ask yourself whether or not you should take advantage of dropshipping. As with any other business model, there are pros and cons. Let's see them now together:

## The advantages of dropshipping

### 1. Low costs

Dropshipping has some advantages, especially for those who are starting their own business and do not have a lot of capital.

In fact, as already mentioned, this business model does not require the products to be purchased in advance or even having to have a warehouse large enough to contain them.

The parties involved in this distribution model are three in total:

The seller runs the online store and tries to win over as many customers as possible. After receiving an order, he contacts the supplier and sends them the order and customer details.

The resulting profit from this transaction is the difference between the amount the supplier charges him for the product and the amount the seller charges his customer.

The supplier, or dropshipper, receives the order and sends the product directly to the customer. On the package there are usually no references to the supplier, only the seller's brand (but not always).

The supplier takes care of all formalities relating to shipping, customs and distribution costs.

The customer buys a product in an online or offline store without knowing if it is dropshipping or not.

Having only contact with the intermediary (the online seller) he does not know who the supplier is.

As soon as the customer has ordered and paid for the product on the online shop, the seller purchases the product from the manufacturer or supplier, and indicates the customer as the recipient.

The advantage is savings: in this case the goods do not have to be purchased and stored in large quantities in advance.

This way you won't have to worry about excess products that remain unsold accumulating dust in your warehouse.

Thanks to the low costs that come with this possibility, the sales opportunity offered by dropshipping is a practical way to test the terrain of e-commerce for those who have just started a business.

## 2. It is not necessary to have a warehouse

Another advantage of dropshipping is that you can offer a wide range of products even if you have a small warehouse, since the goods do not have to be placed there.

It is not even necessary to have a warehouse; all you need to manage your orders is an internet connection.

While this business model offers some excellent advantages, the disadvantages are not lacking ...

# The disadvantages of dropshipping

## 1. Customer satisfaction

With dropshipping, the seller has little influence on customer satisfaction - this is by far the biggest drawback of this type of e-Commerce.

It doesn't matter how good a store's products are, if the supplier doesn't send the package on time, if the shipping takes too long, if the product is damaged or if worst case doesn't arrive at all, your online reputation will be a lose out.

Solving the problem is difficult if you do not know where the goods are currently located and the supplier cannot be reached. Often the simplest option is to agree to refund the customer.

## 2. High shipping costs

Another disadvantage is that when you offer goods from different manufacturers or wholesalers and the customer orders multiple products, it can happen that the shipping costs add up.

In this case you have two options: either you charge the customer for the shipping costs (who will most likely abandon the purchase) or you pay most of the shipping costs.

## 3. Low profit margin

Which brings us to the next, perhaps most significant drawback: the low profit margin.

Even with the prerogative of finding a supplier who offers affordable prices, to generate a significant profit you will need to offer your products at a very high price. But your competition is likely to offer the same product at a lower price, thus winning your clientele.

**There are two solutions to this problem:**

- invest time and money in marketing and branding, build a circle of loyal customers.
- if you can find a good supplier, you can also decide to specialize in a niche market. Typically, if there are fewer competitors selling the same products as you, you can make a higher profit.

## In which sectors can dropshipping be used?

This sales method is possible for almost all types of businesses. Here are some ideas:

On an online store, this sales method is mainly used because it is a great option for e-Commerce companies, as the necessary processes are greatly simplified.

In addition, the manual labor of the seller is reduced to a minimum.

In marketplaces (such as Amazon or Ebay) this strategy is also used by a large number of online merchants. Online marketplaces have the advantage of having a huge circle of customers, which ensures that the products can be seen by a large number of buyers.

At the same time, it also has the disadvantage of playing on "foreign land". You can define your own rules in your e-Commerce, but in a marketplace, you need to stick to the existing rules.

For example, if you sell on Amazon, you will have no influence on the appearance of the package or it is also possible that you may not be able to sell certain products depending on the category of products or the country in which you want to sell them.

**Tip**: Keep in mind that marketplaces aren't free. For the sale it is necessary to pay a commission or even an additional monthly fee.

In local or physical stores, the practice of dropshipping is spreading more and more. Rather than keeping all products in stock, in these stores, customers can choose their purchases by choosing from display items or browsing a catalog.

These products will then be ordered and shipped by the supplier. For example, a furniture store can display a lamp or sofa without needing to have them in stock. This saves on storage costs and avoids shipping bulky goods like these.

## How to get started with dropshipping

The first thing to do should always be this: find the right products and the right supplier.

Once you have finished your search and decided on a product you will need to contact the manufacturer. Even if the manufacturer only sells the product in large quantities, in most cases you will receive a list of wholesalers offering the product or otherwise sending a sample.

Contact the wholesalers on this list and find out which is the most suitable for your project.

There are a number of suppliers and markets that can help you find the right inspiration for any future products you can ship. Some are free, but most are only available for a fee.

## Advice:

Before offering the product in your online store be sure that it is a quality product and that it fulfills what it promises!

Order one first to test it. This way you will avoid annoyed customers. In addition, you can also photograph or make unique videos for your product pages.

Stay up to date on all the new product trends and experiment with new marketing strategies (for example by collaborating with an influencer).

Equally important is cooperation and information exchange with the supplier or manufacturer of your dropshipping products.

Ask questions and try to find out as much as possible about the product to always be one step ahead of the competition and, if necessary, to obtain preferential treatment.

If possible, visit the production site to get an idea of who the manufacturer is and the people behind the product.

## How to choose the right dropshipping provider

The first decision to make after choosing this type of business is to choose a good supplier. After all, it is the supplier who largely influences the satisfaction of your customers, as they must ensure that the products arrive on time and in good condition.

So how do you find good dropshipping suppliers? Below we have collected some aspects that you should take into consideration during your research:

## 1. Complete catalog with constant updates

There are dropshipping suppliers that specialize in some sectors and others that offer a more complete catalog. Depending on what you want to sell you can choose one or the other.

If you choose a wholesaler with a catalog that includes different types of products, you won't need to go to new suppliers in the future if you decide to expand the category of products you offer.

In addition to the diversity of products, it is important to choose a company that recognizes the latest trends and regularly updates its catalog.

Internet sales are heavily based on products and viral streams that can emerge as quickly as they disappear. Think Fidget Spinner!

In this perspective, having a dropshipping supplier who is willing to address these temporary trends is important.

## 2. Different synchronization options

One of the main factors in working with a dropshipping provider are the various synchronization possibilities offered. There are indeed many aspects that need to be synchronized (purchase orders, catalog, inventory, etc.)

The most rudimentary method is the CSV file format, but it involves effort and manual labor that many sellers are happy to do without.

For this reason, some suppliers offer several options: from those that require some technical knowledge (such as an API to automate synchronization) to already existing and synchronized dropshipping shops.

## 3. Barrier-free customer service

Make sure your supplier offers good terms and is transparent when it comes to responding to incidents, defective product shipments, or handling returns and canceled orders.

Depending on where you sell, it can be important for you to choose a wholesaler who offers multilingual customer service.

## 4. Multiple shipping options

Dropshipping makes it easier to sell overseas.

If your dropshipping supplier ships to multiple countries, the geographic factor won't be an issue to worry about.

We therefore recommend that you look for a dropshipping supplier that has agreements with several transport companies and that will allow you to sell in multiple countries.

Don't forget, however, that selling in a new country also requires commitment on your part: you will need to translate your website and define a sales strategy focused on a different culture!

## 5. Products in accordance with the law

A product that is legal in one country is not always legal in another (think for example CBD oil).

To prevent shipments from being blocked at the front because they are deemed dangerous, or even incurring legal consequences, always make sure that the products are legal in the country of destination.

## 6. Warranty

Check the warranty time according to the laws of your country. Usually by law a time is established, in many countries of two years within which the product can be replaced free of charge.

## 7. Provide good customer support

Returns are also part of e-commerce and it is important to think about them in advance. If there is a problem with the customer's order, it is important that your supplier offers you a solution in time.

Returns in dropshipping are usually paid by the supplier, who must accept the return without penalty. Look for a supplier who satisfactorily covers this, so your customer doesn't get the wrong impression and you don't have to worry about it.

In any case, the details regarding the return policy must be present on your page (in the Terms and Conditions).

## Conclusion

Dropshipping offers advantages and disadvantages, but at the same time it also offers huge potential to win large numbers of customers, generate solid revenue, and grow your store.

Especially for newcomers to the world of e-Commerce, it is a good opportunity to gain a first experience and save.

# How to Succeed in Dropshipping

How to achieve success with Dropshipping: in this chapter we will tell you about the steps to follow to achieve satisfactory results in this type of digital business.

Many people ask us every day how to take their first steps in the world of dropshipping, but their fear often and willingly is to try their hand at studying this type of business.

First of all, let's start by telling you that the e-commerce world is by far one of the most explosive business models out there today.

The growth of social media, online shopping, digital payments, artificial intelligence, the world of big data is literally revolutionizing activities and businesses around the world.

The world of dropshipping is obviously reaping huge benefits from this revolution, gaining a rise on a global scale.

It has enormous growth potential, is extremely easy to manage, is scalable so it can allow you to generate profits potentially without any limits.

**Warning**: don't get us wrong! To obtain these results, study, application and constancy are required.

However, we can guarantee you that it is not absolutely impossible anything else.

Now stop chatting, from this moment on we advise you to pay absolute attention, because we will show you exactly what are the 20 steps that have allowed many of us to achieve success with Dropshipping.

## Step 1. Market analysis

A Dropshipping project must necessarily arise from these questions:

- Can I run a dropshipping business?
- Who will be my suppliers?
- Will I find customers to sell my products to?
- What do I need to start my business?
- What are the skills I need?

Asking these questions is crucial to achieving success with Dropshipping. Without understanding these answers, it is impossible to move forward.

You have to do research, define your goals, opportunities and challenges to take.

## Step 2. Learn from competitors

This is a great challenge to face.

No e-commerce owner will openly tell you that it is dropshipping.

Regardless of whether it is dropshipping or traditional e-commerce, it is still possible to draw some teaching ideas that you can reapply to your business.

It is very useful to learn to understand what the product advertising strategies are, how competitors manage ads and social pages, especially if you are a beginner.

Learning from those who are already operating in this type of sector is really very useful.

Looking at how others behave you can really learn a lot, and we are not talking about copying but about getting ideas to improve.

It is very useful to understand how our competitors behave, for example in terms of promotion on social networks.

## Step 3. Choose the right suppliers

To create a dropshipping store, you will obviously have to take care of finding the best suppliers available.

Our advice is to rely on the Aliexpress platform for this type of search.

In our view it is absolutely the best platform for those who want to embark on a path in the world of dropshipping, for practicality, ease of communication, product quality and costs.

## Step 4. Know your interests

It is really much easier to manage a store inherent to your interests, there is no denying it.

**Attention**: we are not saying that it is not possible to do it within a niche that you do not know or that does not represent your direct passion, but it will certainly be a little more complicated for you.

This is because if you have knowledge of the topic dealt with in your niche, you will be able to more easily recognize what are the elements of value to offer to your potential customers.

You will be able to identify the best products to market, using qualitative and high-level descriptions.

You will be able to answer even the most technical and complex questions that your customers will ask you and it will be much easier for you to identify all those elements to use to have a better grip on the public.

## Step 5. Define your target audience

Who are your potential customers?

This is one of the most important questions you will need to know how to answer in order to achieve success with Dropshipping.

This type of knowledge will allow you to promote and advertise your store effectively, providing what is needed in the best way to your target audience.

## Step 6. Exploration of social networks

It is no coincidence that even the largest companies on the market invest hundreds of millions of euros in Social Media Marketing.

You must be able to make the most of the communication channels available to you.

It is essential that you acquire the correct command of online advertising channels and especially of social networks such as Facebook and Instagram.

*"What channels do my potential customers prefer? Blogs, forums, social networks?"*

For example, if you know that your target is mainly on Facebook, then you will need to focus your attention on advertising on this platform or on joining Facebook groups related to your product niche.

## Step 7. Researching the niche on Aliexpress

The selection of the niche on which to base your business inevitably passes from the analysis of the trendy product categories, and in this sense, it is really essential to search for the most marketed items by e-commerce giants such as Aliexpress.

Within this platform you will find all the information that will allow you to make a targeted and thoughtful choice on the products to be marketed in your store.

To understand if a niche can actually be profitable, you need to be aware of what your product really has to offer to the target audience.

You are rightly asking yourself, "And how can I understand it quite safely?"

The product you are analyzing must have certain characteristics on the Aliexpress platform:

- High number of orders on Aliexpress (at least 300);
- Positive feedback in terms of product quality (we recommend focusing only on products from 4 stars onwards
- Good supplier reviews.

These three elements can already give you an idea of the value offered by the niche to the target audience.

Obviously not the only factors to be taken into consideration, but they will allow you in the first place to get an idea of the quality and marketability of the product.

This type of evaluation can also be done in the same way on other platforms such as Amazon, Ebay, and our advice is to focus on the searches carried out on all these platforms.

## Step 8. Evaluation of the potential of the marketing

"Do I have the opportunity to promote the chosen niche through social networks?"

*"Can we study and apply strategies to increase our authority in the eyes of search engines?"*

*"Is it still a profitable niche in the face of paid advertising investments?"*

It is essential to have the answers to these specific questions, in fact the practicability of promotion and marketing strategies will allow you to acquire many more customers, and therefore to earn much more.

To achieve success with Dropshipping it is very important to have a "customer-oriented" perspective.

We need to make the user experience as satisfying as possible, thus guaranteeing a fast, quick and pleasant site, good customer service and prompt response to requests.

## Step 9. Buy quality hosting and domain

We always recommend that you rely on Siteground.

The platform offers in a single solution Hosting, Domain and WordPress installation in 3 simple clicks.

Another invaluable value is the customer service offered by Siteground.

## Step 10. Creation of your e-commerce

If you want to start in this type of activity, we strongly recommend that you start right away!

Alidropship, unlike services like Shopify, will ask you for a one-time payment for the plugin or turnkey e-commerce.

Services like Shopify instead require a monthly payment, with the big disadvantage especially at the beginning of finding yourself at a loss when you will not be able to place sales.

With Alidropship, once you have purchased the service for the first time, you will not have any further costs towards them, except for further additional services that you can request at your discretion.

**HOW DOES DROPSHIPPING ACTUALLY WORK?**

Ok, we talked about strategies, choice of niche, promotion and creation of e-commerce.

But how does dropshipping work? At first glance it may seem complicated but we can guarantee you that it is not at all.

The next steps you will see concern the operational activity of the dropshipper once the e-commerce is built.

## Step 11. Choice of products to import into your e-commerce

Quality, technical characteristics, specifications, prices are all factors to consider when choosing the products to import into your e-commerce.

Carefully analyze all these factors using one of the most powerful tools to carry out this type of evaluation: customer feedback.

Reviews can actually give you even more precise indications than supplier descriptions about product quality.

It may also be useful to buy a couple of products yourself to actually understand if the items offered by a particular supplier are actually qualitative.

Once identified, you can proceed with their import into your store.

With the Alidropship plugin the operation will take place automatically.

## Step 12. Choice of suppliers

The role played by suppliers is absolutely crucial to success. Always consider that the physical product will never touch your hands, you are not the one to manage time and logistics.

Customer satisfaction necessarily depends on the good work of your suppliers.

Through Aliexpress you have the possibility to contact them directly and access their status data completely free of charge.

In this way you will be able to analyze with your own eyes the performances and the feedback released to the supplier.

## Step 13. Entering Orders to the supplier

When you receive the purchase order in your store, all you have to do is pass the shipping information directly to your supplier.

## Step 14. Management of critical issues on orders

It may happen that customer enter some incorrect data. They may mistakenly provide the wrong name or surname or for example shipping addresses.

Sometimes they will change their mind about the purchased product and ask you to refund them.

Or because of their inability to trace the order they will accuse you of having lost it.

In this case it is really crucial to always remain calm and polite.

We are all human and these things can happen in any type of business.

You will always have to give your best to offer solutions to your customers for any type of need.

## Step 15. Implementation of SEO

The "Search Engine Optimization" better known as SEO is a resource that can contribute to the visibility of your e-commerce within the network, in particular in the list of results proposed by search engines.

If you are able to implement SEO strategies correctly, you will be able to benefit from the results in the long term.

## Step 16. Use of social media

Social media are crucial in the development of this type of business. If you are able to effectively promote your products, you will be able to achieve important performances. For example, we have already talked about how to use Instagram shoutouts to advertise the articles marketed in your store for example.

Not least are the strategies based on advertising on Facebook.

If you are a beginner, aiming for continuous publications on Instagram and Facebook is already a good start. From this point of view, it is very important to be constant in your publications trying to involve your users with a "Call to action", or posts that invite surfers to interact with your page.

Example: "Tag a friend who might like ..."

The Call to Action allow you to improve the engagement of your users by allowing you to build a real rotating community on your store, and to create a real brand.

For social publishing you can think of relying on the Social Rabbit plugin which will allow you to automate your social posts allowing you to save a considerable amount of time.

# HOW TO EXPAND YOUR BUSINESS ONCE STARTED

If you are constant and above all with the application of the correct strategies, after some time you should see your business grow step by step and finally achieve success with Dropshipping.

If you stop working especially at the beginning when the results tend to struggle to arrive then surely you will NOT be able to achieve success with Dropshipping.

The beginning is the most difficult part, as in any type of activity, you will have to be patient and work without seeing any kind of result, committing yourself with the sole objective of being able to see things grow one step at a time.

When you finally see the results arrive, you absolutely must not stop, but focus on those processes that will allow you to further increase them.

## Step 17. Improving the customer experience

It is possible to greatly improve the browsing and shopping experience of your customers in your store.

The ease of navigation on your site will entice your users to come back.

Make sure you make payments easy to make, and don't forget to always enter payment conditions, shipping times, return conditions.

It is very important to be extremely honest about the shipping times, they must be absolutely aware of the time it takes to receive the purchased product.

It is not a big deal for people to wait as long as they know that it will arrive.

## Step 18. Product catalog update

Always analyze the sales data of the items, to understand if the products marketed are actually to the satisfaction of customers or if it may be necessary to study a reorganization of your catalog.

## Step 19. Opening of new stores

The launch of the first store is always an opportunity to study the market and acquire those skills that will allow you to really make your own strategies to achieve success with Dropshipping.

Once you have digested this knowledge, why not consider launching new stores?

You will realize with the following launches the enormous number of skills acquired with the first store, knowledge that allows you to achieve the desired results much more easily and quickly.

## Step 20. Explore

There is so much to learn, we guarantee it.

For this reason, once you have acquired your personal experience, you can yourself build new strategies based on your specific history in the business and maybe you can share with the community new winning strategies to achieve success with Dropshipping.

Being Digital Entrepreneurs also means this, a lot, and again a lot of research, testing, development and analysis of results.

# CHAPTER 6 SHOPIFY

If you are thinking of opening an ecommerce or already have one but would like to upgrade, you have probably already heard of Shopify. It is an ecommerce system conceived mainly from the perspective of marketers, therefore characterized by extreme flexibility and ease of use.

## What is Shopify?

Shopify is a "SaaS" (Software as a Service), which is a platform that allows you to create a virtual store in a few simple steps. Unlike a CMS like Prestashop and Magento, or WooCommerce, which is simply a plugin, that is an extension for WordPress, Shopify is a cloud platform that allows you to create an ecommerce without having to install software locally and without needing of a server.

To create your own ecommerce, simply register: the site is hosted on Shopify's servers, a service for which you pay a monthly subscription (we will see the costs of Shopify later).

## 1. Shopify monthly fee

True, unlike the various CMSs for ecommerce, Shopify has a monthly fee to pay. However, this fee includes both the cost of using the platform and that relating to the "rent" of the servers on which your e-commerce is hosted, and this detail makes all the difference.

In fact, CMS like Magento and Prestashop do not offer a hosting service included, which however you need to pay in order to have your own online ecommerce.

The cost of the server, therefore, by choosing to create your ecommerce with a CMS such as Magento, Prestashop or even WooCommerce, must be counted separately, and has an annual fee that with Shopify is instead included in the price.

## 2. Changes to the source code of a Shopify site

The fact that your ecommerce is hosted within the Shopify servers does not mean that you cannot directly act on the source code to make structural changes to your site: the advantage over a CMS is that most of the changes on the user interface side they can be done in a simple way from the editor present within the Shopify back-end, but if this is not enough to satisfy your needs, you can:

- buy apps (often also available for free)
- rely on a Shopify developer partner to make changes to the code of your site (or make them yourself, if you are familiar with programming languages)

Again, the fact that Shopify is a "closed" system is an advantage and not a disadvantage. Maybe the biggest geeks will suffer from not being able to put their hands on the code, but we assure you, from direct experience, that finding a good developer who is able to modify the HTML code of an ecommerce in Magento or Prestashop is not easy at all and that often the damages and the errors that derive from it bring only trouble, rather than benefits.

## Shopify is simple to use

Really. Whatever functionality you want to add, whatever changes you want to make, Shopify allows you to do it quickly and easily in 90% of cases (that is, unless you need to contact a developer).

The app and extension portfolio is vast, as is the choice of themes and layouts to be used, with almost infinite customization possibilities.

With Shopify you can make such a change even on your own: this allows you to focus only on the marketing of your ecommerce, giving vent to your creativity and testing your every idea.

Think for example of the possibility of doing Real Time Marketing: with Shopify in two hours, you can install a pop-up with a flash promo and limited-time discounts, decide which audience segment to show it to, implement a marketing automation workflow in which enter the consumers who join and... earn. Simple.

Shopify is advantageous because it is designed for this: to optimize the management of all the technical aspects to facilitate marketing activities.

## Simple payments with Shopify

Shopify is the only ecommerce platform to natively offer integrations with over 50 of the most used payment systems, a significant difference compared to the most popular CMS for which it is necessary to download an extension for each payment method (Stripe, Paypal, credit card etc.), install it, verify that it works correctly etc.

Shopify integrates and dialogues perfectly with the most used web marketing tools, from the Facebook showcase functionality to the Google Merchant Center of Google Ads, from the Instagram product feed to the most popular email marketing platforms such as Mailchimp.

To connect your ecommerce to these tools, no code knowledge or complex operations are required: a simple click is enough to implement a complete and transversal funnel for online marketing.

Also, not to be overlooked are the integrations, already available in the USA and soon also in Europe, with Amazon and Ebay, to synchronize the showcase, product catalog and stocks between the various sales platforms.

## Shopify is self-updating

Another great advantage of Shopify is the automatic software update: every time a new version is released, your site updates for free and automatically, without you doing anything.

The same is not true if you have chosen to create your ecommerce with a CMS: in that case the transition to the new version must be done manually, moreover the most important upgrades are to be paid for.

## What is Shopify and How does it work

Shopify is, as we said, a SaaS (Software as a Service) platform perfect for building an ecommerce site: all you have to do is register, create an account and start building your ecommerce.

Shopify offers a huge market within which you can choose from a wide selection of themes and layouts, free or paid, available in different configurable and customizable variants with extensions or apps, in order to add all the features of which you need it.

As mentioned, Shopify allows for simple and effective management of integrations with other marketing tools and has the largest portfolio of payment methods, natively available on the platform.

The process of creating an e-shop is very quick and does not require technical knowledge: creating a site is very simple even for those unfamiliar with programming languages and chewing little, in general, on the topic of "online sales".

This allows you to focus only on what's really important to your business and your consumers.

Once you have chosen the template and assembled the eshop thanks to a simple drag & drop editor, you can immediately move on to the operational phase of loading the products.

Another advantage offered by the platform is certainly related to the ease of use of the back as regards the order management phase, which can be carried out from any device, even via mobile app: this aspect allows you to speed up the management times of the order and always ensure maximum promptness in the operation of the aspects related to the sale.

## How much does an online store cost with Shopify?

The answer is: the cost of an ecommerce with Shopify depends on your needs.

It depends on your needs, firstly on how much you are willing or able to invest, on the features you think you need to really take off your ecommerce and your online sales and above all on your turnover, because Shopify holds back a commission on purchases, as we will see shortly.

Don't forget that Shopify offers a 14-day free trial, during which you can use it without purchasing it, to try it out and see if it's suitable for you; later you can choose the most suitable plan according to your needs and change it whenever you want, making a free upgrade or downgrade depending on the market trend and the success of your sales.

Let's see in more detail what the subscription plans are.

## Shopify: the subscription plans

Shopify offers its users the opportunity to purchase 3 subscription plans with different fees, precisely to meet multiple needs and requirements and satisfy everyone, from the small entrepreneur who wants to launch a pilot project of his online business, to the large company that has need more assistance and personalization of their ecommerce.

Shopify Lite is the "beginner" plan that costs only $9 a month and allows you to sell via a social button on social networks, on your blog or on an existing site. It is the ideal choice for those who already have an ecommerce and want to renew it but are not yet convinced to choose Shopify and prefer to carry out a test phase before buying one of the Shopify plans that also allows the creation of the e-shop.

Basic Shopify costs $29 a month and represents the cheapest choice, an efficient entry level from which to start evaluating the potential of the platform. This plan offers all the basic features for selling online and has a 2% purchase commission, which Shopify takes for every product sold.

Advanced Shopify is a solution designed for large businesses. The plan costs $299 per month and offers a series of functions designed to facilitate the management of an ecommerce by a large company, such as the management of 15 accounts. Also in this case, of course, the commission is still lower, dropping to 0.5% for each product sold.

Shopify Plus is the enterprise plan for companies that invoice around 500,000 euros per year. The cost starts from 2 thousand dollars a month but allows you to completely avoid the fee on a single transaction, as well as offering, of course, dedicated assistance, with a team of consultants and technicians always available. This is a higher-level plan that is only suitable for companies with a very high turnover, to justify the payment of such a high monthly fee as a saving compared to the amount of commissions on purchases.

The features between the various subscription plans, especially the 3 central ones which are also the most widespread, are not very different: what makes the difference is the commission withheld by Shopify on each individual transaction, which clearly decreases as the cost of the plan increases.

As we said, however, the subscription is scalable at any time so you can easily start from a basic plan to test the platform and then upgrade if necessary.

## A brief history of Shopify

But let's take a step back and discover the story of this software that is taking the ecommerce world by storm.

Shopify was founded in 2006 as an online snowboard store. The idea of the creators, as stated on their website, was not only to sell products, but to "create our own brand and establish relationships with our customers".

From this concrete need, Shopify was started, which could only be a platform characterized by a strong focus on user experience, marketing and customer care.

The Canadian platform currently has 800,000 active e-commerce stores with a total turnover of 100 billion dollars a year, a network of 5 offices in North America and is rapidly expanding into Asian and European markets.

## Who Shopify is suitable for:

The strong focus on all those aspects related to selling makes Shopify a platform suitable for all those who want to launch or already have and want to improve the performance of an online business.

## Open an online store with Shopify

As we have seen, opening an online store with Shopify is really simple and immediate: there are many examples of business that started from scratch and in a short time have established themselves on digital markets, starting to invoice significant figures.

To open an ecommerce, it is not enough to buy Shopify: you need to have a strategy. Here is a checklist of things to do before launching your virtual store:

- choose and test the product to verify that it is of the expected quality and that it can really have appeal on its reference market (for example on the Italian public);
- choose the business model, which can be B2B or B2C, i.e., sales to other companies or to final consumers;
- identify the supplier or suppliers of the product itself (in case you have chosen to open a dropshipping shop: or of the raw materials you need to make it;
- determine the online selling price;
- create, if you do not already have one, your own brand (logo, coordinated graphic etc.);
- prepare the ground for marketing activities related to product and brand promotion, for example on social networks, through blogs, email marketing and paid campaigns on Google.

## Shopify and dropshipping

Given its ease of use and high performance, Shopify is the tool most used by those who sell in dropshipping.

This is a sales technique that allows an intermediary to sell a product from a third-party supplier without having first purchased it.

The difference with retail is that the initial purchase investment of the product is not required, nor a warehouse: once the product is purchased, it is the same manufacturer, in agreement with the dropshipper, to ship it to the consumer.

The seller therefore acts exclusively as an intermediary between producer / supplier and buyer: it is a very widespread technique especially in the field of import / export, because it allows you to "import" into a market a foreign product that may not yet exist, earning, in agreement with the supplier, with a price increase on the final product which is retained by the dropshipper.

## Web marketing with Shopify

In particular, Shopify allows you to:

- Easily connect social media like Instagram and Facebook and email marketing software like Mailchimp to your ecommerce;
- automatically update the Facebook and Instagram windows and Google Shopping simply by connecting them to the ecommerce product catalog;
- quickly create a list of allowed contacts for email marketing;
- create remarketing campaigns on Facebook quickly and easily by showing users the products they have already seen on your site within the Facebook feed;

- create buy buttons that can be inserted anywhere, even in emails, which link directly to the check out page;
- connect your ecommerce to your Amazon sales channel with one click;
- and much more.

## Doing SEO with Shopify

Shopify proves to be a very performing tool also for doing SEO: first of all, Shopify guarantees a good loading speed of its ecommerce from any device, a determining factor for the indexing and positioning of a website.

Furthermore, the platform provides a series of essential features for making SEO on pages, such as custom URLs, redirect pages, customizable tags etc. The only drawback concerns the inability to access the robots.txt files and the sitemap and the inability to create subcategories.

For the rest, Shopify allows you to implement most of the SEO optimizations that are necessary to correctly index an ecommerce.

## The Shopify blog

Not to be underestimated is the possibility offered by the platform to create a blog within your ecommerce to give a boost to organic SEO and to carry out content-based marketing activities.

The Shopify blog is not as flexible as that of WordPress, a platform that was originally dedicated exclusively to blogging, but it certainly represents a valid tool and a good compromise, especially considering that the blog does not represent the fulcrum around which the activities of sales, but simply an additional promotional and marketing tool.

## Magento

The speech changes slightly if you compare Shopify and Magento: unlike WooCommerce, which is a simple WordPress plugin, Magento is a real CMS with advanced features and almost infinite customization possibilities.

Among the CMS Magento is perhaps the best known and also the most requested by customers who are willing to open an ecommerce with great fanfare, so to speak: it is in fact a professional tool that requires, among other things, the work of an expert developer to be installed and configured.

The advantage of Magento over Shopify once again concerns the economic aspect: the CMS in fact is purchased only once and is not subject to renewal like the Shopify subscription, which can be an advantage, at least in the initial phase.

However, the speech is always the same: if the purchase costs of the Magento platform are then added to those for the creation and personalization of the e-commerce, to be understood in the form of work of a developer, without whom it is impossible to think of creating your own e-shop and the costs for the purchase of numerous plugins and extensions, most of which are necessary to carry out any marketing activity, as well as for a fee, we come to the conclusion that in any case the purchase of a Shopify subscription represents a saving.

## Shopify vs Prestashop

Comparing Shopify and Prestashop you can reach, more or less, the same conclusions as the comparison between Shopify and Magento, with the difference that, compared to the latter, Prestashop presents an intermediate degree of difficulty as regards configuration and use, still remaining an excellent product to create even large e-commerce.

Prestashop also has a completely free version, which however allows you to practically access all the features necessary to build ecommerce.

Furthermore, in recent years the platform has undergone a lot, acquiring an increasingly vast and updated marketplace from which it is possible to download apps and extensions for every type of need, especially on the marketing side.

This aspect makes it a much higher performing product than Magento as regards marketing activities, the only drawback is the presence of numerous system bugs that often limit the functioning of the app.

Furthermore, as with Magento, it is unthinkable to believe that you can create your own ecommerce starting from scratch with Prestashop, as you would with Shopify: to install and configure it, an expert developer is required, the cost of which must be counted, despite the free nature of the instrument.

## Examples of successful ecommerce with Shopify

Aside from the most famous examples such as Kylie Jenner's cosmetics eshop, Daft Punk, RedBull, there are hundreds of small, medium and large companies that have opened a successful ecommerce with Shopify.

# CHAPTER 7 HOW TO MAKE MONEY WITH A BLOG

Is making money with a blog really possible? This is the recurring question that many people ask themselves who, for one reason or another, would like to try to earn money through the internet. The answer is more than positive: it is certainly possible to make money with a blog (even a lot!), But ...

But what the vast majority of bloggers do is not okay. And not because it is difficult to open a blog, on the contrary. Paradoxically, one of the "problems" is that it is all too easy to open your own blogging platform!

In fact, just go to a site like Blogger or WordPress and, with a few minutes and a few clicks, anyone is able to open their own blog at no cost. And now the fun begins (so to speak...). Why?

At this point, the vast majority of bloggers start writing article after article talking about everything that comes into their head. In the meantime, they place banners or AdSense ads and hope, by doing so, to earn a salary or even become rich.

The problem is, if you work so amateurishly, at most you can earn the money to buy yourself a sandwich from time to time. If, on the other hand, you want to earn a real salary, or you want to make some really good money blogging, then you have to get in mind that you will have to work professionally!

This implies certain aspects that you will need to take seriously right away. Let's see in depth what it is ...

First of all, forget about leaning on free platforms! Invest a few tens of euros and buy your own domain name and then the web space on professional hosting, within which you will then install the blogging platform you decide to use.

... Speaking of the latter, many people who are at the beginning often ask me if the blog should be built by themselves, or if it is better to use some CMS.

If you have good technical skills, you can also program the blog yourself but it is absolutely NOT worth it, since there are several free platforms out there that make all your work much easier and that you can use even if you don't know anything about it. HTML, PHP, Java, etc.

That said, you should absolutely use WordPress in what, without a doubt, is the best CMS for blogging that exists. Furthermore, you have the possibility to expand it and customize it to your liking thanks to a huge number of plugins.

Obviously, it's not that you just need to buy a good domain name, a hosting and install WordPress in it to see the money that will literally fall from the sky! The above is just the very first step, which is necessary to get on the web.

After that, the real talk of making money with a blog will be the result of some of your choices and above all of your work. What do I mean? In the sense that, before anything else, you will have to write about ...

## Topics that interest people

If nobody buys a book of poetry in the bookstore, why should they google them and come and read them on your blog? Aside from the usual friend and relative who will pay a visit to your poetry blog to please you, no one else will come!

Ultimately, the first rule that you must follow if you want to make money with a blog, is to publish only and exclusively articles on topics that, even offline, have a large pool of users interested in certain topics.

## Niche topics and profiled users

Always specialize your blog in a niche that attracts. That is, it deals with topics that people are interested in and that, above all, are easily monetized!

The most interesting market niches are those on online loans, mortgages, trading, forex, insurance, physical well-being, marketing and sales (online and offline), relationships between people, business consulting, etc. In short: all those sectors that solve a problem or facilitate the user in some area.

Make sure your blog always covers topics that are part of the same niche. In short:  talking about one thing today and about another tomorrow will ensure that your users, in the long run, will not turn out to be well profiled.

In practice, you will create a pool of users who are strongly interested in a topic and who will follow you because they are interested in how you explain things and possibly solve their problems.

## How to attract visitors to your blog

I'm sorry to disappoint you but, unlike many lies that are heard around, writing good content is not enough to ensure that your blog receives hordes of visitors.

Or rather: this thing was true once (several years ago now!), but now every second tons of brand-new sites and blogs pop up and the competition is very high (especially in some niches!).

Therefore: you either buy the traffic with the various AdWords, Facebook Ads, etc. - but this means investing money (often nota little) - or get it into your head to become a search engine optimization expert

# Make MONEY Online

(also called SEO) and make sure that what you write is well seen and well indexed by engines (Google in the first place!).

Let's be clear: there is nothing wrong with buying traffic, but in this case your blog must have a business model such that what you earn is higher than what you spend on advertising. If not, you make a loss of course.

## Turn your blog traffic into mailing lists

As you may have guessed from what I just said above, getting traffic to your blog costs time, work, and in some cases money. Therefore, it would be a tragedy if these visitors let you escape as they come ...

What do I mean? I mean, you need to have a proven system to periodically bring visitors back to your site. Think what a tragedy if ALL the people who visit your blog never come back! It would mean that you will always have to be bringing new traffic to your web pages... with all that that goes with it in terms of time, work and money.

Furthermore, no long-term strategy for retaining your visitors would be possible. Let alone the eventual launch of any of your new initiatives!

And don't expect people to remember your blog. Or rather: there will certainly be some "returning visitors", but the vast majority of people will never come back to visit you (the web is big and there are millions of blogs and sites!), unless you provide them with a reason.

... And the reason could be a very simple email from you. An email with which: you notify people that a new article of yours has been released, or that from day x to day y you will do a certain promotion, or that on another day you will launch your exclusive product / service, etc., etc.

But how to legally get the email addresses of your site visitors to be able to contact them again when it suits you? It's very simple: give them something interesting in exchange for their email!

For example, if your blog deals with "how to invest in gold", then you could give a special report in PDF (basically a small 10/15-page ebook) where you explain the basic tricks to earn money by investing in gold. In this way, you can build an extremely targeted mailing list for this particular subject ...

To do what I just said in a professional way, there are utilities called autoresponders which, in practice, are programs that will help you semi-automatically manage the list of emails that surfers will leave you in exchange for the gift you give within your blog.

## Monetize your blog visitors

If you do not have a very busy blog, it is useless for you to hope to earn with AdSense or with banners which, to become truly profitable, need very large volumes of traffic.

On the contrary, even a few daily visitors, if well profiled and well followed, can make you earn interesting figures. 100 unique visitors per day - an easy enough traffic volume to reach for a professionally managed site - means you can count on 3,000 monthly visitors. This number could guarantee, for example, 200/300 euros per month.

How? If in your blog you are dealing with a niche and highly profitable topic, such as investing with forex, then you could write reviews to facilitate sales through affiliation to a course on forex trading.

Since a similar course costs around 300 euros per copy and the average commission for affiliates is 30%, for each copy sold thanks to you you could earn around 90 euros.

You can convert the 3,000 monthly visitors into about 300 people who will click on the review link (1 in 10 on average). 300 users who click will most likely generate 2 or 3 sales... that is 180/270 euros of earnings.

If instead of using the affiliations you use AdSense, only one in every 100 visitors would click on the banner (one in 50 only if you are very expert in this system!) Which leads to an average revenue of about fifteen euros (considering 50 cents per click).

However, the best way to make money with a blog is not affiliations but the sale of your products and / or services, however this assumes that you have, in fact, YOUR products or services to sell.

For example, if you are a lawyer or business consultant and you manage to attract, thanks to the articles you write, potential customers interested in your issues, then you could monetize by selling your consulting services to these people.

Instead, as far as real products are concerned, you could use dropshipping or better still you could decide to sell your infoproducts which are an absolutely fantastic and truly profitable business model!

Having said that, consider that being a blogger is a real and often full-time job! There are 17 million bloggers around the world and nearly 2 million of them make money. Over 400,000 bloggers manage to earn as much as a salary with their blogs.

400,000 people means that those who earn a salary with blogs are more than those who earn by being computer programmers by profession ...

# CHAPTER 8 SELF PUBLISHING

Making money with self-publishing is the dream of many people and actually it is not an impossible thing if you know this world well, have passion, if you put in the effort and obviously if you also have a bit of luck.

Today self publishing is open to practically all those who want to make themselves known, share their talent and promote their own site and so on, but let's see what exactly it is.

## How self publishing works

Basically, unlike the classic publication of a book or anything else, with self-publication the various expenses are not borne by an external publisher and each process is carried out independently, relying only partially (if necessary) on external professionals. In practice, the drafting of the text, proofreading, binding and any other aspect is performed by the author.

It is a widely used method, especially if we are talking about e-books and currently there are many platforms that allow you to edit a book with self-publishing and make yourself known even when classic publishers are not interested in publishing the writings of certain authors.

In summary, let's say that earning with self-publishing means self-publishing your works and earning from the sales of the same.

## How much do you earn?

Answering this question in a precise way is difficult, if not impossible, as there are all the conditions to be able to earn staggering figures, but you can also earn very little.

## There are many factors to consider to be successful in self-publishing:

Are readers interested in the published work?

Are there many books sold?

Is the profit margin good?

Does it sell continuously?

If all the above conditions are met then you can also earn 5 figures. On the other hand, if you have little success and you publish in disadvantageous conditions that do not allow you to get a high enough sum from each book sold, you can hardly earn with self-publishing.

## Advantages and disadvantages of self-publishing

Surely the opportunity to make your work known, promote yourself for free and the possibility of earning important figures are the main advantages of self publishing, but it is not easy.

Like any other activity, this one also requires commitment and the acquisition of certain skills, moreover it is not completely cost-free. In fact, among the main disadvantages is the fact that often the platforms that, for example, allow you to self-publish your own book and distribute it, retain a large part of the revenues, whether it is a paper or electronic format. Not only that, it must be considered that especially if it is an e-book the prices are hardly higher than 5 euros, so if you remove all the expenses, the author often remains around 1-1.5 euros for each copy sold.

However, if advantages and disadvantages are compared, we can say that making money with self publishing is possible, it requires a minimum investment and this method allows you to be known even if you are totally anonymous in the publishing world.

After having talked about the costs of Self Publishing and having seen what are the expenses to take into consideration before embarking on the path of self-publishing, we also see the flip side, or how much you can earn by self-publishing your books.

Obviously, the income of a self-publishing author comes entirely from the sales of her books. The earnings percentages calculated on the selling price of a book are called royalties, ie commissions.

## How To Maximize Earnings in Self Publishing?

If you have chosen the path of Self Publishing and want to maximize earnings, you must choose the sales channels that guarantee you the highest royalties.

This too, in fact, is one of the advantages of Self Publishing, because an author who is published by a publishing house signs a contract with the publisher according to which he always earns the same (low, very low) percentage on each copy of the book sold, regardless of the sales channel used.

As a self-publishing author, however, you are free to decide which channels to use, in which online bookstores to sell your book and which intermediaries to choose.

My advice, of course, is to publish directly in bookstores, where this is possible, precisely to get the highest commissions, and use a brokerage platform only to get there where it is not possible to arrive independently.

Direct publishing certainly requires more work, because you have to open an account in each library or platform and repeat the publishing procedures several times. This, however, is the only disadvantage, if we can call it that, of direct publication.

The advantages, on the other hand, are the possibility of controlling all phases of the work, having a faster service and obtaining higher earnings.

## What Is the Best Strategy to Earn More with Self Publishing?

The best strategy to earn more with Self Publishing is therefore to publish your book directly whenever you can and rely on brokerage platforms only to get to online bookstores that do not allow direct entry.

To increase your income with Self Publishing, follow these 5 steps:

### 1) Publish your book in ebook format on Amazon by signing up for the Kindle Direct Publishing program.

Registration is free, as is publication. If you already have an Amazon account with which you shop, you can use that, otherwise open one dedicated to your business as a writer.

### 2) Publish your book in ebook format on Kobo by directly enrolling in the Kobo Writing Life Program.

Registration and publication are completely free.

### 3) Publish your book in ebook format in all other online bookstores through the mediation of a Self Publishing platform.

To see your book put up for sale in all other libraries, where direct publication is not possible, you have to go through the mediation of a platform for Self Publishing, sometimes called aggregator for Self Publishing.

One of the first platforms for Self Publishing was Lulu, which exists and works very well even today, but has an interface only in English. Other consolidated international realities are Draft2Digital and Smashwords, but also with an interface only in English.

### 4) Publish your book in print format on Amazon by signing up for the CreateSpace program.

Once your book is published in paper format, Amazon will link it to the already published ebook format, so that both options will be present on the product presentation page and readers can choose which one to buy.

When a reader buys a hard copy of your book, Amazon will activate the Print on Sale service, print that single copy and ship it to the customer.

### 5) Print your book in paper format with a Print on Demand service.

By printing hard copies of your book with a Print on Demand service, you can sell them directly to your readers during literary presentations.

By following these 5 steps, you will set up the best strategy for your Self Publishing, because not only will you cover all distribution channels, but you will get the highest commissions from each.

So, let's see how much you can earn from each of these services, so you will understand why I have proposed them to you in this order.

## What Are the Author Earnings on Amazon Kindle Direct Publishing?

When you publish your book in ebook format on Amazon KDP you can earn 35% or 70%, depending on the selling price of your book.

The 35% choice is always available, for any sale price.

The 70% option is only available if the selling price of your ebook ranges from $ 2.99 to $ 9.99.

This is why I advise you to carefully establish the price of your book, because your earnings can also depend on this.

Schematic:

- 35% option: valid for ebooks with a selling price from 0.99 to 215.00 euros;
- 70% option: valid for ebooks with a selling price from 2.99 to 9.99 euros.

(As you can see, the minimum price that can be set on Amazon KDP is 0.99 euros. In reality, then, with the promotion functions, you can also set your price at less or even for free.)

Seen in progression, the situation is this:

- if your ebook is on sale with a price ranging from 0.99 to 2.98 euros you earn 35%;
- if your ebook is on sale with a price ranging from 2.99 to 9.99 euros, you earn 70%;

- if your ebook is on sale with a price over € 9.99 you earn 35%.

Do your math well and evaluate if it is really convenient for you to sell your ebook at a very high price.

By setting a selling price below 9.99 euros, you actually earn more, both because you stay below the psychological threshold of 10 euros and sell more copies, and because you are entitled to 70% commissions.

If you can then set the price of the ebook format of your book between 2.99 and 9.99 euros, so you will earn more!

What Are the Author Earnings on Kobo Writing Life?

Also, on Kobo Writing Life the commissions for the authors are divided into two bands, depending on the selling price of the ebook.

Kobo offers you:

- a 45% option, for ebooks with a selling price from 0 to 1.98 euros;
- a 70% option for ebooks with a selling price of € 1.99 upwards.

(In order to take advantage of the 70% option, the price of the ebook must be at least 20% lower than the corresponding paper format, if it exists on the market).

Seen in progression, the situation is this:

- if your ebook is on sale with a price ranging from 0 to 1.98 euros you earn 45%;
- if your ebook is on sale with a price ranging from 1.99 euros upwards, you earn 70%.

## What Are the Earnings for The Author on Streetlib?

As I have already said several times, the passage through a brokerage platform is a necessary step to get to where it is not possible to go alone.

Streetlib offers you a one-time royalty of 60%, regardless of the selling price of your book.

In any online bookstore reached by the Streetlib circuit you decide to put your book on sale, Streetlib will therefore pay you a 60% profit on each copy sold.

The only limitation is for the Google Books store, for which the commissions are lower, but for which Streetlib raises the selling price of your book precisely in order to guarantee you an always equal 60% profit from that bookstore.

To better understand this mechanism, consult the details provided by Streetlib.

As you can see, then, publishing your ebook on Amazon or Kobo through Streetlib (or another intermediary) is not worth it at all!

By publishing on Amazon and Kobo through Streetlib, in fact, you can earn 60% of the selling price of your book, but by publishing in the same bookstores directly you can earn 70%!

In fact, no Self Publishing platform will be able to give you 70% for books published on Amazon and Kobo, because from the royalties guaranteed by Amazon and Kobo, they must deduct a percentage for the service they offer you.

So, of the 70% offered by Amazon, Streetlib takes 10% and gives you 60%, YoucanPrint keeps 20% and gives you 50% and so on ...

The 10% difference may perhaps seem little to you and you might think that - out of laziness - it is not convenient to open many accounts and you can be satisfied with doing everything with a single platform, such as Streetlib.

But I invite you to reflect. As things stand today, Amazon is certainly the most important online bookstore on the landscape. This means that most readers who buy books online buy them on Amazon. But, consequently, this also means that most of the copies you will sell online will be sold right on Amazon!

So why should you lose (at least) 10% on each book sold in the sales channel where you will sell the greatest number of copies?

**There is really no reason.**

Numbers in hand the solution is very clear: publish directly where you can to get the greatest earnings, otherwise part of your earnings will go to pay for brokerage passes that you do not need.

## What Are the Author Earnings on Amazon CreateSpace?

When you publish your print book on CreateSpace, Amazon gives you 60% of the sales price, minus the out-of-pocket printing expenses Amazon has to incur to print copies of your book in Print On Sale.

In this case, therefore, your commissions do not depend on the selling price of your book, but it is obvious to print a bigger book will cost more and, for the same selling price, you can earn more with a book with fewer pages.

During the publishing phase, the Amazon CreateSpace system will immediately calculate how much it will cost to print your book so that you can establish an appropriate selling price.

Schematically, Amazon CreateSpace guarantees you:

- 60% on the selling price of your book in print
- minus 0.60 euros per copy (Fixed Charge)
- minus € 0.012 per page to be printed (Per-Page Charge)

## What Are the Earnings for The Author with Print on Demand?

When you print hard copies of your book with a Print on Demand service you have to anticipate the cost of the entire order. For this reason, I advise you to order from time to time a number of copies that you actually need.

It is useless to fill the cellar with boxes of copies of your book that you do not know if or when you will sell.

However, printing copies of your book is necessary for many reasons, one of which is certainly to sell them to readers directly or during presentations.

Since this is a direct sale managed by you, try to get the maximum possible profit by printing your copies with the Print on Demand service that offers you the best quality / price ratio.

You will certainly need to offer readers a quality book, printed well, on adequate paper, with a strong cover and good binding. You also need to set a cover price in line with the market, otherwise readers won't buy your book.

But once you've established all of these criteria, look for the printing service that offers you the best price.

For example, if you set a selling price of 12.90 euros, which is a low price for a paper book, and then you can print it for less than 3 euros per copy (which is very feasible if it is a book with a text only content, without images, to be printed in monochrome), then you will earn about 10 euros for each copy sold, corresponding to a commission well over 70%.

From this simple example, you understand that selling hard copies of your book directly to your readers can lead to interesting earnings and can represent the highest revenue item in your Self Publishing budget.

As you can see, therefore, the earnings of Self Publishing basically depend on the selling price of your books and the distribution channels chosen.

Now, however, you have no more excuses: don't get fooled and don't leave your earnings to others.

You have all the elements to organize a winning and profitable Self Publishing strategy.

# CHAPTER 9 EARN SELLING ONLINE VIDEO COURSES

The Internet represents a milestone from any point of view, an innovative tool that allows people to always stay in touch, to access information of any kind immediately and to work in a practical way. In this regard, online video courses began, very useful tools that make learning, contact between student and teacher, etc. easier. Not only that, it is also possible to earn money by selling online video courses: a profitable and not binding activity.

## What is a video course?

As can already be deduced from the terms "video course", these are courses available in video format, or multimedia contents that are distributed via the web, capable of replacing the old teaching methods.

Here are the benefits they offer to students and teachers:

The student has the opportunity to follow the course in question where and when he wants, without upsetting his routine. In fact, he can review the course as often as he wishes and generally spends less than he would have to shell out to take a live course.

The teacher, through the creation and distribution of an online video course, can achieve greater notoriety, increase their earnings, decide when and how to organize the course, create a community, etc.

## Topics on which to make a video course

To earn money by selling an online video course it is not necessary to be a luminary, as you can also create a course to teach and spread a passion, just as you can teach a trade. In fact, in addition to the video courses that contain educational material, there are those of sewing, modeling, on how to use certain web programs, etc.

## Where to sell video courses

Teachable: all-in-one platform that manages everything you need to be able to create and sell an online video course, including payments and customer service. There is a free package and others for a fee, starting from a minimum of 39 USD / month.

Newkajabi: perfect platform for those who want to manage a blog and sell online video courses. Pricing: Starting at 103 USD / month.

Udemy: online learning platform that currently has more than 80,000 courses and is among the most complete from every point of view. Course prices start at €9.99.

Academy Of Mine: little-known e-learning platform in Italy that is also used to learn how to develop a video course and that provides everything you need to know about it.

Thinkific: platform that provides the necessary tools to create and market video courses, directly from your website.

LearningCart: e-commerce platform that also specializes in the sale of online video courses, available from 179 USD / month.

Ruzuku: everything you can use to create and market quality video courses. Very interesting especially if you are still unfamiliar in the field.

## How to promote a video course

Those who want to earn with an online video course cannot help but think of a promotional campaign and the most popular platforms are: Facebook (ADS), promotion through YouTube videos and Email Marketing, however also Twitter, Instagram and others methods can be used to make your course known.

## How much do you earn by selling online video courses?

Online we can find video courses that cost a few euros, to even get to some expensive solutions, which can exceed 1000 euros. Based on the type of course that is created, its characteristics (length, quality, notoriety, etc.) you can decide the price and understand how much you can earn by selling video courses.

It is important to use social media and other channels to advertise the sale, thus increasing the chances of good marketing and consequently optimizing earnings.

Create, sell and earn with online courses: we can confidently say that in 2020 this business had an international boom.

Undoubtedly this supersonic increase is a consequence of the health emergency that we are still experiencing worldwide today: it has pushed thousands of companies in every sector to bring their training online so as not to stop their business during the hard months of lockdown (we also talk about it here and here).

Investing in the creation and sale of online courses and in e-learning is an emerging trend both among new realities and among companies that focused everything on being present in the classroom.

Creating a successful online course means having identified a knowledge gap in a certain sector and being able to fill it quickly.

Furthermore, always behind the push of the pandemic, more and more people seem to prefer for their personal training the comfort and flexibility of a study method that allows them to learn not necessarily inside a classroom: but from their homes, during a trip by train, or on a weekend of bad weather.

And this new emerging culture is the perfect ground for the growth of the e-learning industry.

If you have strong industry expertise and aren't selling online courses yet, you're missing out on a great opportunity.

Be among the first to create online training courses in your niche and you won't regret it.

## Earning with online courses: all the variables

There are so many factors to consider when creating your online course: the earnings you can get from selling it can vary a lot.

It all depends on how much care and energy you dedicate to your online courses: do you want to work to make it your core business or will it remain a part-time marginal business? What goals do you set yourself?

Creating an online course is a tiny part of the whole process. The secret to solid income is a lot of work in marketing, sales and above all on your personal branding.

## How much can you expect to earn with an online course?

This aspect varies a lot. You will have to consider a lot of factors that can affect your earning potential.

## The pricing of the course.

Are you selling a 5- or 500-euro course? Proper pricing makes a huge difference in how many people you'll need to reach your earning goal.

## Your audience.

Do you have an email list? Social media followers? A YouTube channel with many subscribers? Do you have contacts with partners and their network of contacts? Put all these evaluations on paper to understand how much you can earn with online courses: the larger and engaged your network of contacts, the more online courses you will sell immediately.

If you're starting out now, building an email list is the first step to building a new online course business.

## Experience in marketing and sales.

Have you started a business before? If you have already started a business in your life (online or not) and you have sold products before, you certainly have an advantage and you can expect a greater conversion from your contacts right away. Your past mistakes and your successes make a difference.

The loyalty of your current contacts. How close and affectionate are they to your brand? Do they come back to you after purchasing your services and products or do they disappear? Do you have a customer base who are engaged?

If you are starting from scratch don't worry: all the points above can be learned. But you definitely have to expect and aim for a slower start than someone who already has some of these aspects.

Now we come to the point: how can you calculate your potential earnings? You will need this formula:

*Earnings = Audience x Conversion Rate x Course Price*

If you don't have an audience yet, you can make some assumptions and predictions based on how many people you expect to reach. Will it be 100, 200 or 1000 subscribers?

Conversion rates to earn with online courses then depend on the subject, the price and above all on your ability to attract and sell to the right people.

To understand if you are making money with online courses, you can consider these conversion rates:

- Low conversion: 0.1% up to 1%
- Average conversion: 2% up to 5%
- High conversion: 6% up to 10%

You can understand what you need to start by doing the calculations on all three conversion rates (1%, 5% and 10%) and study the different scenarios by seeing what goals you need to set in order to achieve them.

Then, if you want to analyze the generation of real profit, you will have to subtract the expenses. One of the advantages of creating online courses is that you don't need huge expenses to get started and above all the expenses of your online course do not increase with each additional customer, as happens for classroom courses.

However, you must consider the costs (even if low) of production and above all the costs of marketing and sales.

This is the calculation you need to do:

*Profit = income - costs (production, marketing, other)*

Now you can really calculate with safe formulas if your online courses can bring you profit and above all make an immediate forecast of what you need.

Increase the value of an online course

There are certain ways to increase the value of your online course.

Some factors affect the value of your courses and you must put them "on the plate" before starting your business, along with those presented in the previous paragraph.

## The strength and notoriety of your brand.

How recognizable, memorable and visible is your brand (which can be your business or your figure) on social media and on the web? For a quick check, we suggest you google your brand name and see what the top search results are.

## Your level of expertise in your industry.

The more knowledge you have in your field, the more you can create high quality online courses and the easier it will be to be recognized as an expert in your field. Be warned, though: You DON'T have to be THE MOST EXPERT to sell with online courses. You just need to know 2-3% more than other people who are dealing with the topic of your online course.

## The amount of training content you already have in hand.

It depends on the amount and variety of educational content you have already created over time to share with your customers and prospects (e.g. blog posts, books, videos, webinars, podcasts, guides and ebooks).

## The topic of the course.

A successful online course begins with choosing a winning topic. The topic of your course determines whether your audience will benefit from it or not, and whether you can sell enough. The quickest and most effective way to pick a successful topic is to ask your audience what information gap they feel they have in your area of expertise.

## The size of your audience.

Having a large number of followers on social media already, an important list of email contacts or old customers and prospects interested in your expertise is important. Course creators with already strong audiences (such as professionals, bloggers, companies, people with authority and celebrities in their industry) have an edge over others when they start opening their own academies online.

There is no question: brand recognition helps drive sales.

## The habits and characteristics of your audience.

Consider how much the target you target earns on average and how much they are willing to spend on average on digital products, such as online courses. There are certainly sectors and professions that, by nature, are more inclined to make money with online courses.

## The key question of your ideal customer.

Before designing an online course, it is very important that you ask yourself this question: would anyone pay to learn more about that topic taught by ME? If so, how strong is that person's DESIRE to do so? Asking these questions and being able to find an answer will be one of the key factors in determining the pricing of your online course and will give you an answer on the level of quality your online course will require.

## The size of the market and competitors.

Think about how many people need your courses in your niche (a solution to a common problem) and especially how your competitors are using this information. Doing a benchmark survey is critical to determining if there is a real market for the online course you have in mind.

## The effectiveness of your site.

Do you own a website? How do people get to your website and how do they interact with your pages (landing pages, sales pages, etc.)?

Working to improve these factors will go a long way in promoting your online course business and gaining greater exposure in online communities, with the goal of selling your courses.

Pro-tip: Your online course business doesn't need to be your earning core right away. You can start this business as a small side project until you start earning your first income - only then will you decide whether to move your businesses and your main sources of income entirely online.

**But can you REALLY make money with online courses?**

The answer is yes. Online courses offer one of the best business models for digital entrepreneurs.

Demand is on a growing trend and people, today more than ever, are motivated to pay for online training, from home, tailored to their own pace. Today, a business based on online sales is one of the most effective methods of making money online.

# CHAPTER 10 HOW TO SELL HANDICRAFTS ONLINE

Thanks to the web, in fact, both artisans and hobbyists, and amateur crafters can put their handmade productions online and make their creativity and skills a job that can create income. However, to sell handicrafts online and make it a profitable business, it is not enough to be a skilled crafter of handmade objects.

To be known, to sell and to have satisfied customers, you need resourcefulness, knowledge of various issues related to the world of online shopping, shipping and even a bit of luck. Except for factors related to luck as an end in itself, in the course of the chapter we will see what are the things you need to know to create the favorable conditions to start selling your creations online, so as to increase the chances of success of your craft business.

If we exclude the variables related to the product itself such as the type of goods for sale, the quality of manufacture and the actual demand for your creations, we can sum up the things to take into consideration to start selling handmade online in:

- How to be in good standing to sell online
- Where and how to sell: the choice of the platform
- The strategic role of shipments and the human factor
- Packaging to protect your creations

So, whether you produce clothing, accessories, jewelry, custom products, diaries, design objects or anything else handmade, get comfortable and discover with us everything you need to consider to sell handicrafts online.

## How to be in good standing to sell handicraft products online

Before understanding where and how to sell your handcrafted creations, it is essential to make some brief tax clarifications on online sales. In particular, it is important to clarify that:

Selling online, regardless of whether it is a professional or occasional activity, is a commercial activity and therefore has limits and requirements to be respected, and tax obligations.

To sell online, there are mainly two methods that we can define as usual, with a VAT number, and occasionally, without a VAT number.

## Usual sale: with VAT number

If your idea is to make crafts your main source of income, and therefore start a habitual sales business, you will necessarily have to go to an accountant to be able to take advantage of the particular tax regime dedicated to small businesses such as artisans.

You must also know that the presence or absence of a VAT number limits you on the tools that you can use to sell online, as the obligation to open does not depend exclusively on the income that this business produces.

For example, if you want to sell through an eCommerce site or a showcase site in which to display products and prices, you must get a VAT number and fulfill all the tax obligations related to it.

## Occasional sale: without VAT number

Opening an eCommerce without a VAT number, we have seen that it is not possible, but this does not mean that selling online is an activity forbidden to those who do not have one. In fact, thanks to the Internet, it is possible to make your creations known and trade them in different ways, as long as you adhere to very specific rules and limits.

The first thing to keep in mind is that the online business you want to start is of an occasional nature. This means that sales must be carried out occasionally and without temporal continuity and, above all, that the income generated by the activity does not exceed 5,000 euros per year. Furthermore, creative work must not be structured and does not require the presence of collaborators.

As for the taxation linked to the occasional sale, you must know that, even in the absence of a VAT number, when you sell an object, a generic non-fiscal receipt in double copy must be prepared, one to be delivered to the customer and one to be kept and presented at the tax office, as the income generated by your creations must be declared.

This brief excursus regarding the rules for selling handicraft products online, without contravening the Italian tax rules, is just a hint of what the regulations on trade are.

To have a more in-depth and exhaustive view of the variables, our advice is to contact an accountant. Only by relying on a professional will you be able to have a precise picture of your specific situation and therefore be able to sell your works without incurring problems and tax penalties.

## Where and how to sell: the choice of the platform

Selling handcrafted products online can give you great visibility and generate opportunities as a result. The web, thanks to the many trading possibilities it offers, has now become an indispensable showcase for anyone who wants to generate profit from their skills, without having to make the large investments necessary to open a physical store or to increase the sales of an already established shop.

The first step to start showing and trading your creations is to choose which tools or online places are at your disposal to create a showcase that could also allow you to export to international markets and therefore to sell abroad. More precisely, the options available to you to sell handicraft products online are:

- Own website
- Marketplace
- Social media

## Own website

Opening a property website is one of the first things you think about when choosing to sell online. Having your own eCommerce, or a showcase site, allows you to sell products without intermediaries and commissions and, consequently, to have complete management of the entire sales process, as well as being able to customize and make your online store unique.

As we have mentioned, this option is only feasible if you have, or are planning to have, a VAT number. However, a proprietary eCommerce, on the one hand, allows you to have the complete management of your business, on the other it requires a fairly expensive financial commitment and specific technical skills, such as: programming, graphics, knowledge of tools for positioning on search engines (to be found) and many others. All skills that you can hardly develop on your own.

A proprietary website is therefore a good solution, if you have the necessary skills to manage it independently, or if you have the necessary capital to entrust these creation and management operations to others, so that you as a craftsman can dedicate your time to creation of products to be sold.

## Marketplace

The marketplaces are virtual places that we can define as the digital alternative of shopping centers. Places where space is rented and, in some cases, even free of charge and where people who visit it can see your shop window and buy products. Amazon and eBay are marketplaces.

The role of the Marketplace is therefore to act as an intermediary between seller and customer, in most cases taking a percentage of the price of what is sold. Obviously, relying on a Marketplace reduces your autonomy, as each platform has its own rules and display windows set, as well as reducing the net income for each product sold.

On the other hand, using one or more of these places to sell handmade products online has a lower cost than opening a proprietary eCommerce site and will allow you to have greater visibility to a site, blog or page about main social networks.

## The main and useful marketplaces for selling handicrafts are:

Etsy: it is the best platform to sell handicrafts, as it was created with the aim of offering space and visibility to crafters who produce handicrafts or sell vintage goods. Given the verticality, Etsy allows you to intercept people interested in buying unique and handmade products. The operation of this website is very simple: you register as a seller, open your shop and you can immediately start uploading the artifacts to the shop. To use it, Etsy charges an insertion fee of $ 0.20 per uploaded product and transaction fees: 5% of the shipping cost shown for the item and 5% of the total item costs (item plus shipping).

MissHobby: Italian website, like Etsy, this portal has a verticality on the purchase and sale of handcrafted creations, creative material and vintage items. To open a shop on MissHobby, you just have to register and pay the annual fee. This Marketplace offers two types of subscriptions: basic, at an annual cost of 12 euros and a commission on actual sales of 3.5% on the price, and a premium profile with a fee of 39 euros per year and a commission on sales of 5 %.

Blooming: is a social commerce platform not specialized in craftsmanship that allows you to create eCommerce without having the skills of a webmaster, at a cost of 9 euros per month and with 5% commissions on sales. The strong points of this Marketplace are the simplicity of creating and managing the store and the possibility of integrating the shop into other channels such as Facebook commerce, web eCommerce, and blog eCommerce widgets.

Amazon Handmade: the online sales giant has added a section and community dedicated to handmade items to the classic Amazon sales for companies and individuals. On Amazon Handmade they can only sell artisans and not retailers of handicraft products. For this new sector of intervention, the colossus of Jeff Bezos has canceled the monthly cost of 39 euros of the Professional sales plan, making the creation of the store and the publication of products on Amazon Handmade free with a 12% referral fee applied to the total paid by the customer. In addition to Handmade, you can use Amazon in its classic version, where you can open a shop both as a professional seller and as a private seller.

## Social media

Until recently, social media was a place used by companies, brands and artisans as a showcase to make themselves known and promote their products, but now some of these social media have evolved and, from a simple showcase, can be exploited as real tools in which it is possible to finalize the sale. We are talking about Facebook with Marketplace and Shopping and Instagram with shopping tags.

These two social networks that are connected, as they are administered by the same company, allow both individuals (always respecting the rule of occasionality and the earning ceiling) and companies to sell what they publish in the feeds of their profiles, without it being necessary leave the platform. Instagram in particular, given its inspirational vocation, is a channel through which to make oneself known and through which to finalize sales.

## The strategic role of shipments and the human factor

If you have decided to sell handicrafts online, you need to know that your work will not be limited to shaping your unique creations. When you decide to start any trading activity, both online and offline, remember that the product is just one of the many things you will have to devote time and attention to. We've already seen that there are several platforms for networking your artifacts, and as you may have guessed, doing so takes time. You will have to take the photos, upload them to all the platforms you have chosen to use, create product descriptions, define prices, advertise yourself, share your products on social media, reply and manage the messages you will receive, prepare the packages, pack them and ship them.

The activities in which you will be engaged will be many and each of these will contribute to the success or failure of your business. The activities of promotion and publication of the articles will allow you to gain visibility, contact with people, since you ship together with the quality of your handcrafted product, instead they will contribute to building a good reputation.

In particular, shipping plays a strategic role in what is called the customer journey. Packaging, shipping and the way in which the shipment will take place are factors that influence the success of the sale and post-sales feedback.

The shipping methods, according to various studies on consumption habits in relation to online purchases, highlight how shipping costs perceived as too high and slow delivery times lead to the abandonment of the cart and how non-delivery, delay or receipt of damaged shipments considerably influence the seller's perception in terms of seriousness and attention to the customer and his purchase.

The choice of the forwarding service is therefore a major problem for anyone who works in the world of sales. To sell handcrafted products online, you must know how to navigate the rates and the many services that couriers provide. To understand who to entrust your handcrafted creations to, it may be useful to use a shipping comparator, so as to find the best service at the most convenient rate in a few, indeed very few, clicks.

When looking for the carrier for your sales, also remember to check what are the additional services offered that can be useful to an online sales activity. For example, for your eCommerce or shop on a Marketplace, it may be useful to have a shipping partner who allows you to offer:

Shipping insurance: subscribing to insurance will ensure that in the event of unforeseen events dependent on the carrier, this will compensate you for the declared value. This stipulation is particularly useful if you are shipping valuable and / or fragile items.

Pay on delivery: this type of service allows your customer to pay for the purchase directly to the carrier upon delivery. Although it may seem an obsolete method of payment, there are still many people who prefer to pay cash on delivery.

Integrating logistics management files with the shipping platform: managing shipments can become complex when you have to send numerous packages, which is why some shipping services allow their customers to integrate store and shipments through plugins and csv import interfaces.

In addition to a punctual and precise shipping service, today users expect polite, exhaustive interactions and able to establish one to one relationship. For the artisan world, the human and relational factor is even more important. Whoever buys from you, will ask you questions about the materials, the creative and realization process, will try to establish a direct and more intimate relationship and in many cases, you will be made personalized requests.

Therefore, to better manage customers, it is necessary to show your passion also in communicating with them, trying to adopt a professional and at the same time human communicative approach, listening to the person requesting information, understanding their needs and an active and concrete attitude in case of problems on orders and deliveries.

The memory of an experience and a pleasant exchange leads customers to leave positive feedback, to talk about your products to friends, to recommend them and share them on social networks; in other words, to create a satisfied customer. And a satisfied customer is the premise of a loyal customer.

## Packaging to enhance and protect your creations

When a sale is concluded, you usually think that you have finished the job and that it is enough to call the courier to whom you have decided to entrust the shipment to collect the package and have it arrived at its destination. In theory this is the case, but in reality, instead, dwelling on the care of packaging helps to make the shopping experience positive.

Careful packaging increases the perceived value of the product and its creator. Until proven otherwise, we live in a visual world and, whether we like it or not, we judge what we experience first of all with our eyes. When preparing the packages to be sent to your customers, you must create packaging capable of protecting the contents to their destination and that at the same time reveals the care that is expected from a person who deals with handmade items and to make people perceive your customers who are important to you and who with their purchases contribute to the realization of a dream.

So, you need to be careful:

The packaging, which has the function of making your creation attractive and attracting the attention of customers. Personalize the packaging with your logo and contact information. Also, research or create packaging that enhances your products, that is original and captivating. Try to insert, for example, in an envelope or on cardboard all the information that could be useful to describe the characteristics of the product, the instructions for use and the indications for taking care of it (washing, in the case of clothing).

The packaging, which has the function of protecting what you have sold along the way: from your studio to your customer's home. For packaging, try to use mostly double-wave cardboard boxes and, if you produce small items, padded envelopes.

## In conclusion

To sell handicraft products online, you have to take many things into consideration: first of all, you have to evaluate whether the activity you want to undertake will be continuous or occasional. All subsequent decisions will depend on this choice, as there are substantial differences at the legislative and regulatory level.

Regardless of how you approach the world of digital sales, as a craftsman, the choice of channels through which to make your creations known will guide the type of sale and the commitment necessary to carry it out.

What you have to keep in mind is that beyond the initial investment for a proprietary platform, the costs necessary to use third party spaces, rely on social networks or use multiple modes together, you will always have to provide a budget for advertising, because the web is a highly competitive territory and to give visibility to your creations, it is essential to invest in communication, campaigns on search engines and sponsorship on Marketplace and / or social networks.

Once you have visibility, remember that you must commit the same energy and care that you put into creating your artisan products in the processes of contacting customers and shipping, because, as we have already said, these are elements that, if neglected, risk invalidating the effort put into forging your ideas and promoting them.

# CHAPTER II BECOMING A SOCIAL MEDIA MANAGER

*Working from home in the digital world: because it is a choice that pays off*

Since the beginning of the current health emergency, many companies have adopted new smart ways of working and have approached digital, and this makes experts in digital marketing and writing for the web, but also social media managers, increasingly in demand. In our opinion, there are three advantages of working digitally:

- it is the future of the world of work, given that digital is constantly evolving and is modeled on the basis of the needs of the company;
- the demand exceeds the number of specialized figures in the digital field that exist today and there are many experts in the field of SEO, SEM and ecommerce sought by companies all over the world. Yet, there are very few real experts trained and with valid qualifications in the sector.
- it's a job that allows you to travel, since working digitally means having only a computer and an Internet connection. For this reason, most of those who work with and on the web are freelance professionals and belong to the much-envied category of "digital nomads".

## 5 good reasons to become a social media manager

Now that you understand the advantages of working in the digital world and on the web, let's see the 5 reasons to become a social media manager, one of the most requested professions by companies of all sizes.

1. It is a real and stable job, unlike what most people think, as long as the professional has a specific role and advanced qualifications. Knowing how to use social media is not enough, it is about studying marketing and communication to listen to the target, plan digital strategies tailored to the company and increase brand engagement.

2. It is a job for those who fear boredom, as it is creative and unpredictable. Social media is, in fact, a relatively new world, but above all changing and malleable. For this reason, becoming a social media manager is the ideal choice for those who have a creative personality, love to work in stimulating sectors and seek continuous evolution. In a world like that of the web that runs at the speed of light, the social media manager knows how to keep up and is in favor of change.

3. It is an interactive job, as the social media manager is in contact with the outside world more than you might think. In particular, it constantly studies the environment to influence and direct user decisions, leading them to comment, interact with brands and make informed purchasing choices.

4. It is a job for those who love to make predictions about the future, since in social media marketing it is important to anticipate fashions and trends: knowledge here must be in real time if you want to always be one step ahead of your competitors. Constantly updating means growing from a personal and professional point of view, to always offer customers the latest news in the sector.

5. It is a job linked to the field of marketing, given that the goal of those who want to become social media managers is to make a brand or an activity known to the public to whom it is proposed. Of course, like all marketing jobs, patience, persistence and perseverance are required to achieve the desired results.

Those who want to become social media managers do so to establish a relationship and an active relationship between customers and the company, increase brand awareness of the brand, listen to the public and above all sell products and services directly through social channels or through word of mouth.

Not only that: social media marketing strategies must be integrated with other online and offline marketing initiatives, to create a unique synergy capable of leading to the achievement of the desired objectives.

The social media manager (SMM) is a new but already well-established job in the communication sector, who deals professionally with digital marketing and specifically with social media marketing.

More and more companies have within them an expert who takes care of marketing campaigns on social networks, or to rely on an external consultant who works as a self-employed worker.

Social media managers are highly sought after nowadays and more and more skills are required of them, as they have to deal with diversified strategies designed according to the target and the social network in which they work, which is often not just one, because companies prefer to be present on as many platforms as possible, depending on their digital communication strategy.

We are therefore talking about a very competent professional figure, who in his training touches different areas of digital marketing, moreover he must be prepared with regard to the functioning of all social networks, even the less known and emerging ones.

All this is very different from declaring oneself a user and enthusiast of social media, as many of the youngest people can be, since claiming to be a manager of these platforms means knowing their secrets, functionalities and above all knowing how to organize content to be published on social networks

To summarize the work of an SMM we could say that it creates content, a publication plan and manages social networks also from the point of view of comments and the community.

First of all, every social network manager studies his client, listening to the objectives that the company wants to achieve, the target it addresses with its products and services, the competitors with which the client competes on the market and in general how it wants to structure the social marketing campaign. It is then up to the SMM to develop a real strategy in line with the client's requests and which is subject to the budget made available by the latter.

Once all the important and fundamental information has been established, the social media manager must draw up an editorial plan for the publication of the contents on the various social networks on which he wants to operate. This tool is very useful to an SMM, as it allows you to keep an eye on the periodic publication of contents and their management in a better way.

The so-called editorial plan is nothing more than a planning usually drawn up on an Excel spreadsheet, where the social media manager starts planning the contents to be published on the platforms already a week or several months in advance, taking into account holidays, particular recurrences that you want to remember, and other important occasions for the customer's business.

From the editorial plan, the editorial calendar is obtained, where not only the days of publication and the connected contents are established, but also the times, the format, the text and the relative images are decided.

At this point we must take care of the creation of the contents that we want to publish on social channels. These must be absolutely original and the social media manager will have to study them on the basis of the customer's activity, any products or services sold, or taking into account the audience to be reached, trying to stay in line with the values and the brand image that you want to communicate.

An SMM therefore also deals with the creation and realization of texts, images and videos that are descriptive and captivating, but also optimized according to the social network on which they will be published.

Precisely due to the diversity of activities that an SMM has to face in his work it is usual that this is compared and supported by other professional figures, such as copywriters who write texts, or video makers and graphic designers who instead create the multimedia content.

But what does a social media manager do besides planning and creating content for social networks? There are at least two other tasks that are up to this figure and which are subsequent to the creation of content: the first is the mediation of comments under the posts or statuses published on social media and, in general, the management of the community.

The public is the one who decides if a content is successful or not and, consequently, if the work of the SMM has been adequate, so it is important to listen to its needs and understand their tastes. It is precisely in carrying out this latter task that the figure of the social network manager meets that of the community manager, that is, a professional assigned solely to the management of a virtual community such as the one that is being formed by the visitors of a page on social media, especially when this starts to be very popular.

Usually, the community manager takes care of involving users, asking and answering questions, all according to the tone of voice agreed with the customer and also in line with the image that the brand wants to give of itself.

However, there is another task that falls to the SMM and that is to manage the advertisements related to social media, the so-called social media advertising, an area in which many specialize because companies often look for experts in the field.

Online advertising is important because on social networks the visibility of posts is linked to algorithms that vary continuously, which can penalize or favor a certain type of content or page, so a good social media manager must also sponsor the contents that shares, in order to ensure maximum visibility and reach as many people as possible.

What an SMM does and whether his work is professional can also be assessed by the insights, visible within the different social networks, which the same social media manager analyzes to understand the progress of his work.

## The salary of a social media manager: how much does he earn?

Becoming a social media manager is a career option that attracts many people, especially young people who are passionate about social networks and new technologies, because they feel very comfortable in these digital contexts, even if it is possible to undertake this training path at any age.

The attractiveness of this job also depends on the fact that it is a very requested job nowadays: almost all companies, even the smallest ones, want to have an account on at least one of the main social networks, and to do this they must contact an external smm for advice or hire one.

Before embarking on this career, it is good to actually figure out how much money a social media manager makes. We have already highlighted that an SMM has many skills precisely because it has to fulfill different tasks, not always similar to each other but also quite diversified, but what is the salary of a social media manager ultimately?

First of all, it is important to remember that some SMMs work as freelancers, i.e. with a VAT number, and offer advice to many customers, or others are regularly hired within a company or communication agency, working exclusively for this and sometimes also fulfilling to jobs that are slightly outside of strict social media marketing.

In general, however, a good SMM with a few years of experience and an adequate cultural and training background can earn about 30 thousand euros a year, which can increase.

In case you prefer to work as a freelance SMM, the average salary will certainly be difficult to calculate with certainty, as it depends on many variable factors, the first of all is the number of commissions that you accept or for which you are requested, and also the extent of these.

It is clear that the more customers you have, the more a smm will earn at the end of the month, but the quantity is not always a guarantee of a high salary, this is because the remuneration established for a service varies according to what needs to be done: is it a question of managing a single page or multiple accounts, within more than one social media? This is already a fundamental difference, since in the first case the work is less demanding and therefore also less expensive, while in the second we are faced with a complex and certainly more profitable project.

Whatever the job that you will have to fill, it is good that a freelance SMM establishes with each client what his consultancy will consist of in a specific way and does it before starting the job. You will have to decide with the customer how many pages to manage, how much content to publish weekly, how much to invest in advertising and other details.

Based on this, the consultant's earnings will be established, often on the basis of a price list that he has drawn up for each different job based on his competence, work experience and professionalism.

Some SMM freelancers prefer to receive an hourly wage, based on how long it takes them to complete the various tasks agreed with the client, rather than obtaining a fixed salary. Everyone has an hourly rate that can range from 10 euros, if the job is rather simple or the social media manager is just starting out, up to 50 euros, if the SMM is in great demand and the work is complex.

The only problem with being a freelancer is that, especially at the beginning of their career, a social media manager will have to seek out their first clients and make themselves known. Many social network managers use social media to highlight their work and their professionalism, with pages on the various platforms that are used as a portfolio of the various projects completed.

Another very different case is when the social media manager works only for a company and within it, as an employee in all respects. In this case, the SMM will have a pre-established salary fixed according to a contract, as happens for any other type of worker.

The amount of the salary will vary according to the skills of the hired subject, his experience and obviously also according to the tasks that he will have to carry out, and therefore objectives to be achieved in terms of visibility or social pages to manage.

Sometimes a social media manager also takes care of other tasks when he is hired full time by a company, which go beyond the traditional tasks, for example he can work on all marketing campaigns, even non-digital ones, or he can take care of communication.

Also, in this case it is evident that it is difficult to estimate what a social media manager earns, since the variables to consider are many. The salary of a social media manager who works as an employee of a company can usually reach over 30,000 euros.

Becoming a Social Media Manager attracts many young people and social network enthusiasts, at ease in these digital contexts, but it is possible to train at any age to start working as an SMM.

In addition to the various skills or duties that the SMM hired can have and cover, an important indicator for evaluating the salary that will be recognized is given by the type of contract that he enters into with the company. A young SMM novice and with less than a year of experience will probably be hired as an intern, earning a salary of less than 1,000 euros per month.

The contractual form may vary, but the intern who after a while has gained experience is no longer considered at an entry level, but more experienced, and therefore his salary will also gradually increase. On the other hand, it is evident that a professional already established in the world of work will be able to obtain a much more substantial salary at the first try, which can even reach several thousand euros per month.

When you ask yourself how much a social media manager earns on average, it is always good to remember that in this job experience counts a lot, and this comes in part from good training, continuous refresher courses and targeted studies, but also from work in the field.

The experience of a young SMM will increase after a few jobs completed, and with this the salary that the social media manager will earn at the end of the month will also go up, regardless of whether he is an employee of a single client or a freelancer who works with several clients.

However, the positive side of working as an SMM is that, although practical experience is fundamental, thanks to a good training course in social media management it is possible to create a solid foundation, to be able to launch into the job market with greater safety.

If you have finished your studies to become a social media manager, but you still have little experience in the field, to acquire the latter and start becoming required even by medium-large companies it will take very little time, if well spent, compared to many other jobs that still require some practice or years of apprenticeship.

Just consider that after a few months of practice you can be hired for a paid internship or start getting small clients as a freelancer, and after a year of work as an SMM you leave the entry level and you can start to consider yourself (and above all to be considered by clients) as a professional.

## How to become a social media manager: the guide

After seeing what a social media manager does and trying to determine what a social media manager's salary is, it's time to get to the heart of the matter and actually talk about becoming a social media manager.

As in all professions, there is no standard and mandatory path to follow, which ensures the same results for all those who pursue it. Every person who decides to become a social media manager starts from a different point than another, both in terms of age, gender or origin, as well as with regard to previous education, attitudes, tastes and passions. Already it is easy to understand that finding a single training path is almost impossible, as well as wrong, as it would not fit everyone in the best way.

We have drawn up several points to help anyone who wants to pursue a career as an SMM to understand if there are fundamental starting requirements, if there are school and university paths that are more consistent than others and to find the easiest way for everyone to become a social media manager.

## The requirements to become a social media manager

As in all jobs and in life, it is always important to remember that everyone is the architect of their own destiny, and that therefore if there is a passion for a particular job or topic, such as that for social media marketing, even if you do not have the skills or aptitudes necessary at the beginning, these can certainly be improved and refined, to reach the final goal.

However, there are obviously requirements and characteristics for being an SMM, which if you already possess them before starting the actual training to become a social media manager, can be useful.

With university courses or training courses you study certain concepts and useful materials in the work of SMM, such as the basics of marketing and communications, but that can be learned by anyone with good will, and there are some features that are part of each person who can be of help for one job rather than another. Let's see together what are the requirements to be met to become a social media manager.

First of all, there are two really important characteristics that anyone who wants to become a social media manager should have: curiosity and perseverance. The world of the web and even more so, social media, are constantly evolving; they live on technological discoveries and new trends, so being curious to discover new things, wanting to always be updated and never stop training is essential to work in this field.

It is not enough to have good character requirements and study the theory, once you have started working you have to continue to inform yourself and update yourself periodically, otherwise you risk becoming obsolete, and to do all this you need an always running engine that can be fueled only by curiosity.

Consistency goes hand in hand with what has been said, since a good SMM is constant in training and practice, which is fundamental in this job, but then remains constant even after starting his career.

In practice, an SMM will never stop studying on a regular basis, so those who want to enter this world must have a clear idea that they will need to study again and again, with determination, passion and constancy.

A fundamental requirement for pursuing a professional career as an SMM is to be passionate about social networks.

A requirement that is fundamental to undertake a professional career as an SMM is clearly being passionate about social networks: the latter are the field of action of an SMM, for which a professional, in addition to having to study and know them in depth, must also be fascinated and find them interesting and inspiring.

To learn the basics of social media management faster, it may be useful to use the main social platforms on a daily basis, perhaps by creating and managing personal pages, even without specific purposes such as product sales or sponsorship, but simply to understand the mechanics of social media and practice before going to manage the pages of future clients.

The work of the social media manager is still part of the great world of marketing, in which a creative and limitless mind is important to be able to see things that others do not see, to understand what the public likes before the competitors and to be able to produce innovative, original and interesting content.

We must not forget that the SMM is a figure that is often confused with that of the community manager precisely because of the activities they sometimes carry out in common: even those who want to become social media managers will have to manage the audience of users who frequent the social pages that they share, try to create a loyal community and interact with it to create a lasting relationship.

Surely to become a good social media manager it is a precious advantage to have strong communication skills, useful both for writing the head-on content of the posts, and for interacting with the virtual community and also finding it pleasant to relate to other users.

## What to study to become a social media manager

We have seen that there are very important character requirements that can make the difference in a career like that of the SMM, but what are the skills to cultivate to become a social media manager?

The attitudes such as perseverance, passion for social media and good interpersonal skills with customers are not enough to make a person a good social network manager, because these intrinsic characteristics should be associated with the technical requirements, which can be acquired only through practice and study.

As the world of social media is increasingly central to everyday life, professional figures related to social media management are spreading rapidly, as are many specific training courses. A person who wants to obtain the skills required to become a social media manager can now choose from a grand and variety of training: universities, masters, targeted courses, etc.

To understand what kind of path to choose and which is the most valid, first let's see together what are the specific skills that an SMM should have, and then understand what are the best training paths to follow to obtain them.

We have already seen how broad this profession is and how many jobs it encompasses, sometimes quite different from each other, but there are skills that are useful in almost everyone, one above all is the knowledge of marketing, since a social media manager works in the field of digital marketing, and more precisely in that of social media marketing.

A good knowledge base of this subject, also in aspects concerning other types of marketing is certainly useful. We then talked about the interaction with the public that an SMM has continuously, for which a preparation in sociology, psychology, communication or other humanities subjects that can help the consultant understand the needs of the users is well appreciated.

Then there are the more particular technical skills, for which theory combined with practice is fundamental. Some bases of graphics, video and photo editing and copywriting are very important to create innovative, original and high-quality content, to be published on the social pages of clients.

Finally, an SMM often faces situations that involve the management of websites, blogs, or advertising campaigns. For all these reasons, the basics of programming languages, even the most common ones such as HTML, web design and SEO (Search Engine Optimization) can be essential to be able to cover the role of a professional and competent all-round figure, increasingly requested by companies.

But where to actually study all these notions? We have already highlighted that there is no single preferable path for everyone, so there is no problem if you are passionate about managing social networks: there is no ideal time to learn the basics, what matters is to train and do a lot of practice.

A good starting point in terms of training, especially if you intend to undertake a career in SMM from a very young age, could be to attend targeted university faculties. These can really be the most disparate: you can enroll in humanistic courses such as psychology, communication sciences or political sciences, or economics and marketing.

But be careful: this is the starting point for forming preparatory bases for work, because after a more generic three-year degree, in fact, many more specific paths will be encountered. Continuing with university you can choose faculties of marketing, digital communication, business communication, since all of these contain exams and subjects useful in the SMM career.

There are more and more possibilities to follow to become a social media manager, precisely because he is an increasingly requested figure, so universities are offering more and more targeted paths, with courses designed to be able to work in the digital field and with social media, for example. Certainly, training of this type is extremely complete, even if it requires years and years of preparation only on theory.

Fortunately, there are faster alternatives, in fact it is possible to enrol in post-graduate courses or masters, which are increasingly specific to degree courses, or to the many training courses that are online and beyond.

Another great place to start is reading: there are so many books and manuals that talk about managing social media and working as an SMM. Surely, they are not comparable to a specific training course, but reading books dedicated to the social network sector is important as an initial approach, to understand if you are on the right path, if we like that world and if we want to continue with more in-depth studies, in which to invest time and resources.

Obviously, you have to choose, and the best of the most recent publications, and training courses, especially those online, often contain the latest news and are updated more often.

## The most important social networks to work as a social media manager

## Facebook

Surely Facebook is one of the social networks that a social media manager uses the most, because practically all companies have a dedicated page here. The work of the SMM in this case focuses on the production of textual or visual content such as photos and videos.

The company pages on Facebook allow you to give the public a lot of information, such as opening hours of a store, contacts, etc, and allow the insertion of a product catalog and the connection with the company website and with other social media. An SMM here certainly has his work cut out in managing a Facebook account on behalf of customers, given the different functions that this social platform offers.

On Facebook, contact with the community is central, which expresses its ideas through the "likes" of the pages or content published, but also by commenting on the posts or by writing to the page in private.

## Instagram

Instagram is another very popular social network especially among young people, moreover it is among those preferred by companies to share information with possible customers. Founded as a sort of virtual and shareable personal photo album, Instagram provides for the inclusion in your account of audiovisual content such as photos or videos, but also of reels (short videos of max 30 seconds) and longer videos in the IGTV section, which can be accompanied by short descriptions, crazy with the hashtags.

In this case, the social media manager must have good creative skills and also understand graphics and photography, to create captivating and unique content. Also in this case, contact with users is essential and takes place through comments and likes, as well as by deciding to follow a page.

Instagram also offers the possibility of creating so-called stories, i.e. visual content available in your profile for only 24 hours, in which through a photo or video the SMM can give more informal and brief information to users, without having to resort to the publication of a post. This is very useful content that allows you to develop new, more interactive forms of storytelling.

## TikTok

Of Chinese origin, TikTok was created to publish music videos and has become very popular all over the world among the very young under 20, reaching over 800 million active users. Hashtags can also be used here to promote content, while users interact with each other by commenting and liking the videos.

Challenges are very common on TikTok, i.e. challenges launched by users in order to spread and become viral: these represent an excellent use by companies to promote a new product, for example. The short videos can be used by SMMs to promote new services or products that the brand places on the market, associating them with challenges to engage and attract new users.

## Twitter

Twitter is really a simple social media, as well as one of the first to be invented. In addition to being intuitive in its use, it also has few features unlike Facebook or Instagram. Although you can post photos or videos on your page, the text cannot exceed 280 characters. A social media manager will recommend this social network to his client companies first of all for the general public, given that Twitter hosts over 200 million users, but also in the event that the company wants to address particular issues or communicate with its target in a more direct way than can be done on other social networks, or to address a more specialized audience in some sectors.

For example, on Twitter there are often public conversations between users, which are accessible and can be commented on by everyone, including experts from different sectors and beyond. The community that is created on Twitter is very linked to the company in question and this is great for an SMM or a brand.

An unusual use for other social media and which Twitter performs for many companies is that of customer service: many companies have made this service available online through this platform, where the SMM responds in real time to users who ask questions about the company's products or services.

## YouTube

YouTube is a social network where users have a channel, within which videos are shared, usually accompanied by a short caption. Inside you will find content on the most diverse topics: from products by professionals to amateur level videos.

Many companies decide to rely on this platform to advertise video content regarding the history of the brand, the production of the products sold, advice on their use, the explanation of the services provided and much more. Like Facebook, Instagram and other social media, on YouTube a SMM can share content to advertise the client company, which will be viewed by users before or while watching videos of other subjects.

## LinkedIn

LinkedIn is mainly known for connecting users within the world of work, and it is also one of the few social networks created specifically for companies. A social media manager can use LinkedIn fi his client is looking for staff, and therefore by posting an announcement of the vacancy on this platform, or to find suppliers of services or essential materials in production. There are really many features that LinkedIn makes available for companies and which, consequently, can be exploited by an SMM or by those who do social recruiting, or those who deal with personnel selection through social networks.

## Pinterest

Pinterest is widely used among DIY, fashion and design enthusiasts, who share their creations and tips for making them here. Surely it is a less well-known social network than the other more famous ones, but it is by no means a platform to be underestimated.

In addition to the large catchment area, Pinterest is excellent for advertising the products of the company for which the SMM works, given that this social network generates greater conversions in terms of sales and purchases, even larger than Facebook and Twitter, if we consider proportionally the number of subscribers.

## Snapchat

Like Instagram, Snapchat was created to share photos or videos, usually by adding special effects to images or voice, the so-called filters that were then also adopted by Facebook and Instagram. These contents can then be shared with the members belonging to a list, so they are not visible to everyone, but it is the user who chooses who to show them to, or they can be shared only with one or a few chosen recipients.

Content posted on Snapchat is only available for a while and then disappears, after which it is unrecoverable. But how can an SMM use Snapchat for his client company?

Surely it is a perfect social network for real time marketing, that is to publish contents that ride the wave of a certain topic that became popular for a short period. Moreover, Snapchat users are above all young and very young, so it is a social media suitable for businesses who sell goods and services suitable for that target or to test new promotional campaigns, which on other social networks would be too visible.

## Telegram

Telegram is a widely used messaging social network in recent years, which allows you to send text, files, audio, video and photos in a very secure and encrypted way. An SMM can configure this social network to communicate internally with the company's employees or externally with the company's customers. Businesses use Telegram, for example, to speak directly with customers as in a customer service or to offer these exclusive promotions and preview news.

## Whatsapp

Not everyone knows this, but WhatsApp is not only an app dedicated to messaging that relies on the internet instead of a text message subscription, but it is also a social network. Although it is widely used in the private sector, for some time this platform has offered a business version of the social media manager, which provides specific features for companies.

# Make MONEY Online

This version is an application different from the one commonly used and is called WhatsApp Business, and after being downloaded it must be configured with a phone number related to the company and by entering the information related to this, as well as the category of the activity which you occupy.

For the rest, the operation is similar to that of classic WhatsApp, but with many additional functions, for example a social media manager responsible for managing Whatsapp Business can set a welcome message that is automatically sent to users when they contact the number of the company for the first time, or quick answers or absence messages for the moments when a shop is closed, all fully customizable.

It is a social medium that allows you to have direct contact with the community and which can also act as a customer service or as a replacement for a newsletter, to make customers receive the latest promotions or news on the company's products.

## Quora

On Quora there is a continuous exchange of questions and answers, where those who answer well can get a score from other users based on the validity of the comment given. A company helped by its social media manager can use Quora to answer questions from customers or interested parties about products and services.

## Tumblr

On Tumblr there are pages of different users structured as if they were blogs, where multimedia contents, texts or animated GIFs are shared. A social media manager can manage a profile on Tumblr on behalf of his client through which to sponsor products and services offered. The great advantage of this platform is the great variability and flexibility, with a wide capacity to adapt to all production contexts.

## vk.com

Aimed mainly at the Russian-speaking community, vk.com looks a lot like Facebook in its setting: in it, you can share texts and thoughts, photographs and videos, and users show their consent by following the pages. Here businesses can create pages and content in the same way they create them on Facebook.

## Weibo

Weibo is very popular in China: in this social network, in addition to sharing the typical contents of other platforms, you can also create small personal blogs. The relevance of this social media for companies lies in the fact that here you can find promotions to buy products online.

## Xing xing-logo

Xing is used as LinkedIn to recruit new hires or find work, it also offers the possibility of communicating with customers, competitors and colleagues, thus creating a circle of interest.

## 4 tips for becoming a social media manager

We have now thoroughly explored the world of social media management, what a social media manager does, how much he earns, how he must train to get good jobs and so on. However, there are still some useful tips to become an SMM that we want to provide to you, in particular we have thought of some really simple but fundamental tips for starting a professional career in the field of social media.

### 1 - Subscribe to the main social networks and become familiar with the platforms

As already said several times, the practice of becoming a social media manager is really important: this can be started even before actually starting to work for clients. As they will be your battleground throughout your career as a social network manager, you should start right from these platforms.

Subscribing to the main social networks can be very useful to start getting familiar with the platforms that will then be used for future customers. Starting to use personal accounts helps you get an idea of how individual social networks work, the differences between them, the type of audience that follows them, the hottest and least suitable content.

### 2 - Try opening an account to launch a personal project

After opening a personal account on one of the main social media, an aspiring SMM can begin to manage their pages, just like they would with those of customers, setting goals to achieve. You can start approaching with the creation of content, to see which formats are most appreciated by the audience of that particular platform, or you can become familiar with advertising, promoting content with paid advertising available in almost all the main social media.

## 3 - Take a training course to learn the basics of Social Media Management

We said it: training is important. By now that of the social media manager is a professional job and suitable only for experienced and competent people, for this reason it is important to study with targeted paths. As already mentioned, there are also many online training courses to become a social media manager, although it is difficult to choose a really good one.

## 4 - Do not stop studying and training yourself

Social media is a new world in continuous and rapid evolution, so even those who work within it must always be updated. To do this, social media managers, even those with more experience and already established in the sector, continuously resort to training, through refresher courses and discovering new frontiers of their work.

Staying informed on current trends, on the new social media that are continuously introduced and, on the contents, most appreciated by the public is essential for an SMM, so that he can offer a service to his customers that is always updated and obtain evident and desired results.

## Extra tip: the main tools for social media managers

Clearly there must be basic skills to carry out the work of an SMM, but to help in the management of social networks there are also tools, specific tools to facilitate social media managers. So let's see the most used tools in social media marketing.

Let's start with Buffer and Hootsuite, which allow the social media manager to organize and schedule the content they intend to publish, creating a single Dashboard. You can manage multiple social networks at the same time and adopt the best format for each.

In the work of social media manager, it is also important to monitor results through the study of data and engagement. Some useful tools in this sense are Chartbeat, which allows you to receive data about shares and audience on social pages in real time, and Datalytics, which allows you to analyze the most important metrics such as the accounts that name the brand, users potentially reached with a content, the number of comments, the total number of views.

Now that you've read our complete guide, including all our tips, you've learned everything you need to know to become a successful social media manager. All you have to do is start studying and start practicing. Good training!